# BIBLICAL
# PERSPECTIVES
# ON
# DEATH

OVERTURES TO BIBLICAL THEOLOGY

A series of studies in biblical theology designed to explore fresh dimensions of research and to suggest ways in which the biblical heritage may address contemporary culture

*The Land*
by Walter Brueggemann

*God and the Rhetoric of Sexuality*
by Phyllis Trible

*Blessing*
by Claus Westermann

*God the Father*
by Robert Hamerton-Kelly

*Editors*

WALTER BRUEGGEMANN, Dean of Academic Affairs and Professor of Old Testament at Eden Theological Seminary

JOHN R. DONAHUE, S.J., Associate Professor of New Testament at Vanderbilt Divinity School

# BIBLICAL PERSPECTIVES ON DEATH

LLOYD R. BAILEY, SR.

 FORTRESS PRESS    Philadelphia

**Library of Congress Cataloging in Publication Data**

Bailey, Lloyd R 1936–
  Biblical perspectives on death.

  (Overtures to Biblical theology)
  Includes bibliographical references and indexes.
  1. Death—Biblical teaching. I. Title.
II. Series.
BT825.B257    236'.1    78-14661
ISBN 0-8006-1530-1

7397L78   Printed in the United States of America   1–1530

In memory of my grandmother,
Lillie Bailey (1886–1974),
at whose death the biblical
faith was sufficient.

# Contents

# Series Foreword

Biblical theology has been a significant part of modern study of the Jewish and Christian Scriptures. Prior to the ascendancy of historical criticism of the Bible in the nineteenth century, biblical theology was subordinated to the dogmatic concerns of the churches, and the Bible too often provided a storehouse of rigid proof texts. When biblical theology was cut loose from its moorings to dogmatic theology to become an enterprise seeking its own methods and categories, attention was directed to what the Bible itself had to say. A dogmatic concern was replaced by an historical one so that biblical theology was understood as an investigation of what was believed by different communities in different situations. By the end of the nineteenth century biblical theology was virtually equated with the history of the religion of the authors who produced biblical documents or of the communities which used them.

While these earlier perspectives have become more refined and sophisticated, they still describe the parameters of what is done in the name of biblical theology—moving somewhere between the normative statements of dogmatic theology and the descriptive concerns of the history of religions. Th. Vriezen, in his *An Outline of Old Testament Theology* (Dutch, 1949; ET, 1958), sought to combine these concerns by devoting the first half of his book to historical considerations and the second half to theological themes. But even that effort did not break out of the stalemate of categories. In more recent times Old Testament theology has been dominated by two paradigmatic works. In his *Theology of the Old Testament* (German, 1933–39; ET, 1967) W. Eichrodt has provided a comprehensive statement around fixed categories which reflect classical dogmatic interests, although the centrality of covenant in his work reflects the Bible's own categories. By contrast, G. von Rad in his *Old Testament Theology* (German, 1960; ET, 1965) has presented a study of theological traditions with a primary concern for the historical dynamism of the traditions. In the case of New Testament theology, historical and theological concerns are rather roughly juxtaposed in the work of A. Richardson, *An Introduction to the Theology of the New Testament.* As in the case of the Old Testament there are two major options or presentations which dominate in New Testament studies. The history-of-religion school has left its mark on the magisterial work of R. Bultmann, who proceeds from an explanation of the expressions of faith of the earliest communities and their theologians to a statement of how their understanding of existence under faith speaks to us today. The works of O. Cullmann and W. G. Kümmel are clear New Testament statements of *Heilsgeschichte* under the aegis of the tension between promise and fulfillment—categories reminiscent of von Rad.

As recently as 1962, K. Stendahl again underscored the tension between historical description and normative meaning by assigning to the biblical theologian the task of describing what the Bible *meant,* not what it *means* or *how* it can have meaning. However, this objectivity of historical description is too often found to be a mirror of the observer's hidden preunderstanding, and the adequacy of historical description is contingent on one generation's discoveries and postulates. Also, the yearning and expectation of believers and would-be believers will not let biblical theology rest with the descriptive task alone. The growing strength of Evangelical Protestantism and the expanding phenomenon of charismatic Catholicism are but vocal reminders that people seek in the Bible a source of alternative value systems. By its own character and by the place it occupies in our culture the Bible will not rest easy as merely an historical artifact.

Thus it seems a fitting time to make "overtures" concerning biblical theology. It is not a time for massive tomes which claim too much. It appears not even to be a time for firm conclusions which are too comprehensive. It is a time for pursuit of fresh hints, for exploration of new intuitions which may reach beyond old conclusions, set categories, and conventional methods. The books in this series are concerned not only with what is seen and heard, with what the Bible said, but also with what the Bible says and the ways in which seeing and hearing are done.

In putting forth these *Overtures* much remains unsettled. The certainties of the older biblical theology *in service* of dogmatics, as well as of the more recent biblical theology movement *in lieu* of dogmatics, are no longer present. Nor is there on the scene anyone of the stature of a von Rad or a Bultmann to offer a synthesis which commands the theological engagement of a generation and summons the church to a new restatement of the biblical message. In a period characterized by an information explosion the relation of analytic study to attempts at synthesis is unsettled. Also unsettled is the question whether the scholarly canon of the university or the passion of the confessing community provides a language and idiom of discourse, and equally unsettled—and unsettling—is the question whether biblical theology is simply one more specialization in an already fragmented study of scripture or whether it is finally the point of it all.

But much remains clear. Not simply must the community of biblical scholars address fresh issues and articulate new categories for the well-being of our common professional task; equally urgent is the fact that the dominant intellectual tradition of the West seems now to carry less conviction and to satisfy only weakly the new measures of knowing which are among us. We do not know exactly what role the Bible will play in new theological statements or religious postures, nor what questions the Bible can and will address, but *Overtures* will provide a locus where soundings may be taken.

We not only intend that *Overtures* should make contact with people professionally involved in biblical studies, but hope that the series will speak to all who care about the heritage of the biblical tradition. We hope that the volumes will represent the best in a literary and historical study of biblical traditions without canonizing historical archaism. We hope also that the studies will be relevant without losing the mystery of biblical religion's historical distance, and that the studies touch on significant themes, motifs, and symbols of the Bible without losing the rich diversity of the biblical tradition. It is a time for normative literature which is not heavy-handed, but which seriously challenges not only our conclusions but also the shape of our questions.

In the present volume Professor Bailey has addressed the problem of death in a fresh and suggestive way, showing how the handlings of death in the Bible have pertinence to contemporary discussion. Given the current rash of theological literature on the subject, it might be wondered why yet another book. However, Bailey offers a perspective which serves not only *(a)* to provide fresh resources but also *(b)* to critique implicitly much of the current discussion as being too thin.

The reduction of the mystery and anxiety of mortality to a psychological, personalistic, and therapeutic problem to be solved is indeed a trivialization of a key human agenda. Whereas death had in the past been treated by a conspiracy of silence, now it is handled in a nearly pornographic way with analysis and resolution. The reduction of this human predicament to the "process of dying" has its most powerful analogue in the reduction of the mystery of sexuality to technique and genitalia. Bailey counters this by attentiveness to the largeness and deepness of the question from which the Bible does not flinch, either by a conspiracy of avoidance or by an overly aggressive resolution.

Bailey's approach is neither an attempt at archaizing the reader back to ancient thought as a way out, nor at contemporizing the Bible to modern problems. But he delicately stays with the texts in ways which move toward the strange meeting of the mystery of death and the consciousness of modernity. That subtleness is apparent (1) in his fine balance of comparative materials and an honest statement about the normative claims of the Bible, (2) in his recognition that the large issue of mortality is not reducible to a concrete problem of "death and dying," and (3) in his sensitivity to the interplay between the biological and metaphorical meanings of death.

Bailey has faced important issues, both substantive and methodological, in a way which makes a significant contribution to the discussion, perhaps contributing to a reorienting of the categories. Finally he requires that death and mortality be discerned as theological issues. And no onslaught of modernity can reduce that reality.

WALTER BRUEGGEMANN
JOHN R. DONAHUE, S.J.

# Abbreviations

| | |
|---|---|
| 1 QH | Hodayot: Thanksgiving Hymns from Qumran Cave 1 |
| 1 QS | Manual of Discipline, Qumran Cave 1 |
| LXX | Septuagint |
| AB | Anchor Bible |
| *AfO* | *Archiv für Orientforschung* |
| ANE | Ancient Near East |
| *ANESJ* | *Ancient Near East Society Journal* (Columbia University) |
| *ANET* | *Ancient Near Eastern Texts* (Pritchard, ed.; 2d ed.) |
| AOAT | Alter Orient und Altes Testament |
| *BA* | *Biblical Archaeologist* |
| Bk. Jub. | Book of Jubilees |
| *BO* | *Bibliotheca Orientalis* |
| *CAD* | *Chicago Assyrian Dictionary* |
| *CBQ* | *Catholic Biblical Quarterly* |
| *EJ* | *Encyclopaedia Judaica* |
| *ERE* | *Encyclopedia of Religion and Ethics* (Hastings, ed.) |
| HUC | Hebrew Union College |
| *HUCA* | *Hebrew Union College Annual* |
| *IDB* | *Interpreter's Dictionary of the Bible* |
| *IDBS* | *Interpreter's Dictionary of the Bible, Supplementary Volume* |
| *IOVCB* | *The Interpreter's One-Volume Commentary on the Bible* |
| *JAAR* | *Journal of the American Academy of Religion* |
| *JAOS* | *Journal of the American Oriental Society* |
| *JB* | *Jerusalem Bible* |
| *JBL* | *Journal of Biblical Literature* |
| *JCS* | *Journal of Cuneiform Studies* |
| *JNES* | *Journal of Near Eastern Studies* |
| *JRH* | *Journal of Religion and Health* |

| | |
|---|---|
| KJV | King James Version |
| MT | Masoretic Text |
| *NEB* | *New English Bible* |
| *NPNF* | *Nicene and Post-Nicene Fathers of the Christian Church* (Philip Schaff, ed. [New York: Christian Literature Co., 1888]) |
| NT | New Testament |
| OB | Old Babylonian version |
| OT | Old Testament |
| *PAPS* | *Proceedings of the American Philosophical Society* |
| RSV | Revised Standard Version |
| SBL | Society of Biblical Literature |
| *SVT* | *Vetus Testamentum, Supplements* |
| TB Shab. | Babylonian Talmud, Shabbath |
| *USQR* | *Union Seminary Quarterly Review* |
| *VT* | *Vetus Testamentum* |

# Preface

Some sections of the present work are extensive expansions of studies that I have previously published: (1) "Death as a Theological Problem in the Old Testament," in *Pastoral Psychology* 22 (November 1971): 20–32; (2) "Mortality and the Fear of Death," *Death and Ministry,* ed. J. D. Bane et al. (New York: Seabury Press, 1975), pp. 252–60; (3) "Death in Biblical Thought," *Encyclopedia of Bioethics,* 4 vols., ed. Warren T. Reich (New York: Macmillan Co., Free Press, 1978), pp. 243–46. Gratitude is hereby expressed to the respective publishers for permission to utilize and expand these articles.

Although the present volume may be helpful to scholars and students in the field of biblical studies, it was not written exclusively for them. It is intended as well for all those persons who sense in the reality of mortality a problem of meaning and who are interested in how some of their fellow human beings have grappled with it. It should be especially helpful for those members of the synagogue and church in the present who acknowledge that the Bible has been and remains formative for their identity. With this wider readership in mind, bibliographical citations (in notes) are often limited to items at the introductory level.

Quotations of the biblical text are based upon the Revised Standard Version unless otherwise specified.

When ancient texts are quoted, material in parentheses generally consists of modern editorial clarifications, whereas that in brackets usually is a restoration of a missing section (lacuna) in the text.

LLOYD R. BAILEY, SR.

# CHAPTER 1

# The Modern Situation

*Indicative of a Universal Human*
*Response to Mortality?*

"It cannot be that I ought to die. That would be too terrible." Thus Leo Tolstoy's fictional character Ivan Ilych apparently sums up the modern response to death.[1] Our reluctance to accept our mortality is evident in pervasive euphemisms,[2] changing emphases in literature,[3] funeral practices that move the family to the perimeter and which disguise reality,[4] impersonal care of and evasive conversation with the dying,[5] ardent hopes that modern medical science will overcome death,[6] the amount of attention given to the topic in recent philosophical writing,[7] and even in the liturgies of the various churches.[8]

Some students of human nature, culminating in modern psychoanalysis, have proposed that anxiety about mortality and fear of impending death are universal human responses. The human dilemma is that we are caught between two worlds, the one symbolic and the other animal; we are able to transcend nature and speculate about the mysteries of the universe—able to experience awe and love, able to create value systems—and yet we are part of a body that aches, stinks, and dies; we are able to soar, physically as well as mentally, among the stars, yet are destined to rot beneath the ground; we are often beautiful of form, yet constrained to bodily functions that shame us: "gods with anuses." This incongruity, it is said, produces a fear of death which must be repressed lest one become mad and which is the common denominator behind many, if not all, other fears and drives.[9]

Such fear and attendant repression are generalized dogmatically by analysts of the highest reputation and following. "At bottom, *nobody* believes in his own death. Or, and this is the same: In his un-

1

conscious, *every one of us* is convinced of his immortality."[10] "The fear of death is a *universal* fear even if we think we have mastered it on many levels."[11]

That the fear of death is not unique to modern persons is indeed evident in earlier art and literature,[12] and it commonly has been projected back into the preliterary period.[13] In the classic articulation of Freud, it was this fear which nourished belief in life after death: unable to face absolute negation, humans, already accustomed to avoidance of stressful situations as a defense mechanism, projected immortality upon themselves.[14] Indeed, the beginnings of religion (theism) itself are often associated with fear of death, as is graphically stated by a character in Dostoevski's novel *The Possessed:* "Man simply invented God in order not to kill himself. That is the sum of universal history down to this moment."

The incongruity of death and human existence is evident in those "primitive" cultures which seemingly lack an awareness that humans are by nature mortal: they need not inevitably die but can only be killed by acts of violence, disease demons, or the evil magic of enemies.[15] And even when mortality came to be perceived as the human condition, the earlier mentality may have survived in stories of paradise lost: humans, perceived to be originally and rightfully immortal, became subject to death only because of the jealousy of the gods or because of human error.[16] Modern persons may be revealing this same mentality when they ask concerning a deceased person, "What killed him/her?" The question seems to presuppose an accidental invasion, an agent from without, rather than an inevitable internal limitation of the creature.[17] Accidents "kill"; diseases "kill": seemingly it is more comforting to perceive them as something that happens to us than as a consequence of what we are.

While this assessment and generalization of the human condition is widely held in the modern Western world,[18] it is not at all clear that it is inevitably and universally applicable. At least the following cautions and counterindications may be mentioned.

1. As a matter of method, can the experience of one society, at a given time and place (i.e., the modern Christian West), be safely assumed to be indicative of humanity in general?

2. Modern Western persons who do not evidence death anxiety, or

fear of approaching death, apparently are not impossible to find. They include some persons of intense religious dedication and those in extreme pain for whom death is a welcome relief. Such absence of fear appears to be evident even in case histories from which psychiatrists have drawn the opposite conclusion![19]

3. Modern Western persons may be a misleading paradigm, since they may feel the threat of mortality more acutely than their ancestors. This is true for a variety of reasons, including:

a. The scientific revolution, beginning in the seventeenth century, removed humans from the center of the universe and undermined their ability to believe in immortality. They could now be seen as inhabiting an insignificant planet in a vast and impersonal universe—as a mere moment in the endless evolution of life. And even when they pridefully came to see themselves as the end product of evolution, their death could seem all the more incongruous.[20]

b. Recent advances in medical knowledge and technology have (1) encouraged the mentality that death is an enemy which can be delayed or perhaps even defeated;[21] (2) increased the life span with the result that death is less frequent and thus is unfamiliar and fearsome;[22] (3) isolated the ill and the dying in special facilities so that they are not part of our social interaction.

c. Modern American funeral practice has transferred the activities and services traditionally performed by family and friends into the hands of professionals, thus further depriving survivors of therapeutic confrontations with the reality of death.[23]

d. Our impersonal city culture encourages relationships that are functional rather than relational and emotional. As a consequence fewer persons experience the reality of a given death. The community is no longer involved in the grieving process. The few true mourners thus feel death more acutely because of their isolation and conspicuousness.[24]

e. Medieval Latin Christianity, with its emphasis upon God's wrathful judgment and its vivid depictions of the terrors of the damned, likely increased the fear which one felt as death approached. Evidence of this reaction may be found both in art[25] and in the widespread desire for a slow death so that one could have adequate time to prepare for the postmortem judgment and hopefully thereby escape the torments of hell.[26] To be sure, there are antecedent emphases in the literature of the Intertestamental period and of the NT (see chaps. 5–6 below), but without the gruesome detail and certitude which characterized medieval Christianity.[27]

Many modern Western persons have found it increasingly difficult to continue believing in a postmortem judgment,[28] and this has had at least two consequences: (1) increased anxiety about the meaninglessness of life: death has become God;[29] (2) preference for a sudden death, since there is no longer need for a preparation time and since one thereby escapes the pain and indignities that can accompany a lingering terminal illness: fear of death has been overshadowed by fear of the process of dying.[30]

5. A substantial challenge to the ubiquitous claim that the fear of death is universal (and is of such severity that it is repressed) is presented by Walter Brueggemann's assessment: within the biblical historical context and faith-understanding, death was "not particularly feared."[31] This challenge is all the more interesting and important since the modern church, apparently largely acclimated to its death-denying cultural context, formally acknowledges the Bible as its canon,[32] that is, as its identity-forming and identity-sustaining narrative.[33]

It is the OT in particular which may form a contrasting interlude between the religions of the ANE and the mentality of the modern West. It perceives that death comes from *within* (i.e., that it is a natural and acceptable condition), whereas its predecessors, contemporaries, and successors propose that it comes from *without:* it is an autonomous (or semiautonomous) divine power (Sumero-Akkadian religion), or an enemy of the created order (Christianity), or an incongruity which modern medical research hopefully will overcome or which indicates the absurdity of the world.

If humans, unable to accept the reality and finality of death, projected immortality upon themselves as a defense mechanism, why did not ancient Israel develop that option? And if a decreasing ability to affirm life after death has nurtured a modern nihilism, why did the OT literature not move in that direction?

It is an answer to such questions, as well as an evaluation of Brueggemann's assessment, that will be sought in the following chapters.

# CHAPTER 2

# Some Perspectives on Death

# among Israel's Neighbors

Ancient Israel's canonical responses to impending death and to mortality can be clarified by comparing and contrasting aspects of them with the responses of Israel's Semitic neighbors. (See below, chaps. 3–4.) Thus it is necessary to begin our inquiry by attempting to summarize the content and mood of the literature of the surrounding peoples as it relates to death. This, it must be admitted, is a hazardous undertaking, given the diversity in style and intention which the literature contains, that its age ranges over two millennia, and that the modern reader's world view likely is vastly different from that of the sources. (For more detailed expression of the difficulties as they apply to the literature of the OT see below, chap. 3, sec. A.3, 5, 6.)

## A. DEATH AND THE DIVINE ORDER
## OF THINGS

According to Babylonian creation stories humans were created in order to maintain the physical world and thus relieve the gods of that necessity. The Atrahasis Epic[1] is illustrative of such thought in the second millennium B.C., if not the third. The warrior-god Enlil, having received the earth as his portion to govern, sets a group of lesser gods to work on an irrigation project. After toiling endlessly to dig out riverbeds for the Tigris and Euphrates, they start to grumble against the management-class gods who dwell in the sky above. Then they burn their tools and surround Enlil's dwelling, demanding relief. Enlil caucuses with the other gods and enacts their suggestion that a human labor force be created so that the gods may be relieved.[2] The

5

birth-goddess Nintur obliges them by mixing clay with the body of a slain minor deity, and thus humans were fashioned.[3]

Similarly, in the epic of creation now known as Enuma Elish,[4] the lesser gods are faced with the task of building a resident-city for the creator-god Marduk. The latter, in order to ease their task, decides to create humans:

> Arteries I will knot and bring bones into being.
> I will create *Lullu,* "man" be his name,
> I will form *Lullu,* man.
> Let *him* be burdened with the toil of the gods,
> that they may freely breathe.

The task was accomplished by slaying a minor god who had instigated a rebellion against Marduk:

> They bound him, held him before Ea,
> inflicted the penalty on him, severed his arteries;
> and from his blood he formed mankind,
> imposed toil on man, set the gods free.[5]

Human purpose and expectation within this mythological framework are entirely this-worldly. The humans are creatures, mortals; their death is ordained by the divine scheme of things. This is aptly expressed in another epic, in response to Gilgamesh's search for a means of overcoming mortality:

> Gilgamesh, whither rovest thou?
> The life thou pursuest thou shalt not find.
> When the gods created mankind,
> Death for mankind they ordained,
> Life in their own hands retaining.[6]

To judge from the surviving literature, the implications of this mythological framework were not always acceptable to those whom it described. There are sustained protests against the general fact of mortality and a vast number of expressions of terror as individual death approached or was anticipated.

Perhaps the most sustained record of revolt against death that has come down to us from the ANE is the Gilgamesh Epic.[7] When the story opens, the hero, a young and energetic king of Uruk, is depicted as so extraordinary that no human is a fit companion for him. He is contemptuous of death, saying that should he fall in combat with a terrible monster named Huwawa, his fame would be perpetuated by poets for generations to come. So self-sufficient is he that he can spurn the advances of a goddess who desires to marry him and easily slay "the bull of heaven" whom the high-god Anu sends to attack him. But when his recently acquired heroic companion (Enkidu) dies, death ceases to be a remote abstraction and becomes his central concern. So unable to accept Enkidu's fate is he that he keeps the body, unburied, until it is filled with maggots. He then begins a quest for a means of escaping death, a quest which takes him to the ends of the earth where he is given the above-quoted observation by a barmaid. There also he interviews the flood hero Ut-napishtim ("the one who found life"), whom the gods had granted immortality—an unrepeatable event, as it turns out. The latter, however, takes pity on Gilgamesh because he has displayed such terror of death: "What can I do, Ut-napishtim? Where shall I go?...The Rapacious One lurks in my bedroom: Death! Wherever I turn my face, there he is: Death!" Gilgamesh thereupon is told the location of a magic plant (appropriately named "elderly man becomes child") which if eaten will rejuvenate one. He secures the plant only to have it stolen by a snake, which then sheds its skin and appears to be rejuvenated.[8] Gilgamesh then stoically resigns himself to his fate, surveying with satisfaction the city which he has built and which will survive his passing.

## B. CAUSES OF DEATH

A sense of the human emotional response to impending death may likewise be gathered from a mythological text.[9] The goddess of fertility, Inanna, has been freed from the underworld so that nature may be renewed, but on condition that a substitute be procured. She chooses her husband Dumuzi because he has not lamented her disappearance. Next comes a description of the activity of the deputies (demons) of the underworld-gods who have accompanied Inanna, and of Dumuzi's reaction. May we assume that what is described is the normal human reaction, projected into a story about the gods?

"The lad—put his feet into fetters (?)
The lad—throw a noose (?) over him, put his neck into the neck-stock."
Hooks (?), awls (?) (and) long (?) needles (?) were lifted to his face.
They gash him with large axes,[10]
. . . . . . . . . . . . . . . . . . . . . . . . . . . .
The lad—they bound his arms . . .
They cover his face with a "garment of fear."[11]

A similar projection of human reaction to death(-demons) may be found in the texts from Ugarit. The head of the pantheon, El (while celebrating a funeral feast?), is described thus:

He drank wine till sated,
Must till inebriated.
. . . . . . . . . . . . . . . . .
An apparition accosted him,
He floundered in his excrement and urine.
El collapsed, El like those who descend into Earth.[12]

The malign forces of disease and death may be divided into three classes[13] and the human response to them may be gathered from their description.

1. *Demons,* residents of the underworld, of which there are several kinds, among them:

a. The *gallu*-demons, often seven[14] in number, described as "full of wickedness"; he "roams in the city, he kills people without mercy"; "the evil *gallu* (that) have come forth from the nether world"; "the spawn of murder, likeness of the evil *gallu*-demon."[15] In the aforementioned story of Inanna, it is *gallu*-demons which drag Dumuzi to his death.

b. The *asakku*-demons, which have given their name to the diseases which they were thought to cause: "Who can withstand the sheen of the *asakku*-demon?"; "an *asakku*-demon overwhelmed (him) like the flood of the river"; "the evil *asakku*-demon in his body"; "I have chased off the *asakku,* the jaundice, (and) the chills of your flesh."[16]

c. The *alu*-demon: "They are charged with terror-inspiring luminescence like the *alu*-ghost"; "who strikes everything like lightning"; "who envelops (his victim) like a garment"; "paralyzed his body like the *alu*-ghost." The term seems to denote a "personal psychic experience often described as a formless and featureless demonic power which engulfs the entire individual."[17]

d. The she-demon Lamashtu, thought to be particularly dangerous to newborn children. Depicted on prophylactic plaques as a lion-headed female with talons and pendulous breasts, she would slip through the smallest opening in a house, find an unguarded infant, and suckle it, leading to its death. An incantation describes her thus: "(her) claws are long. Her forearms are dirty....she has slipped in through the door socket and is about to kill the baby. She has seized (the child) in the abdomen seven times. Remove your claws!"[18] Similar activities were attributed to the female *lilitu*-demon (Lilith: see below).

e. The *ahhazu*-demon, which has given its name to the disease for which it is primarily responsible (jaundice).[19]

f. The *labasu*-demon: "I am the paralyzing *labasu*-demon"; "if he (the sick man) gets the profuse sweat of the *labasu*-demon."[20]

g. The *utukku*-demon, thought to lurk in the desert, around burial places, and so forth, and to attack humans. (The term is also rarely used for the "ghost" of a deceased person, e.g., of Enkidu in the Gilgamesh Epic.)

> Through the gloomy street by night they roam,
> [Smiting] sheepfold and cattle-pen.
> . . . . . . . . . . . . . . . . . . . . . . . . . . . . .
> In the city like a snare they are set,
> Through the door like a snake they glide,
> Through the hinge like the wind they blow,
> Estranging the wife from the embrace of a husband,
> Snatching the child from the loins of a man.[21]

h. The demon Pazuzu, known especially for attacking women during pregnancy and childbirth, and thereafter a danger to the infant. He is depicted as a winged figure with the head of a lion.[22]

2. *Ghosts (etemmu)*[23] of a deceased person, disembodied apparitions who have come out of the tomb or the underworld. If a person had not been properly buried, if food and drink offerings were not regularly provided at the tomb by one's survivors, or if one had died with certain potentials unrealized, then the *etemmu* would roam the earth and attack whatever mortals it might encounter. Thus the

goddess Ishtar, initially denied entrance to the underworld, threatens its rulers as follows:

> I will smite the door, I will shatter the bolt.
> I will smite the threshold and tear down the doors.
> I will raise up the dead, that they may devour the living.
> And the dead shall outnumber those that live.[24]

And Enkidu, the companion of Gilgamesh, trapped in the underworld, arises to describe what he has seen:

> Him whose corpse was cast out upon the plain...
> His ghost *(etemmu)* finds no rest in the nether world.
> Him whose ghost has no one to care for (it)...
> It eats what is left in the pots and other scraps of food that are thrown into the streets.[25]

An incantation lists some of the unfortunate persons whose *etemmu* might roam the earth and be a threat to the living:

> Whether thou art a ghost *(etemmu)* that hath come from the earth,
> ..................................................
> Or a woman (that hath died) a virgin,
> Or one that lieth dead in the desert,
> ..............................
> Or a ghost that none careth for,
> Or a ghost with none to make offerings,
> ................................
> Or a ghost that hath no posterity,
> ..........................
> Or a woman (that hath died) with a babe at the breast,
> ............................................
> Get thee hence![26]

It was the obligation of the deceased person's heir *(paqīdu:* "one who attends to") to provide food and drink offerings by means of pipes *(arūtu)* which extended from the surface into the tomb. An important part of such funeral cults was "calling the name" of the deceased, thus giving psychological satisfaction to the living that they would not be forgotten after death. A related need is attested in the desire of kings for their names and deeds to be perpetuated in writing and in the widespread reuse (in the Late Babylonian period) of ancestral family names.[27] The worst vengeance therefore that could be heaped upon one's enemies was to desecrate their tomb and slaughter their descendants. Thus King Ashurbanipal tells of opening the tombs of the kings of Elam (traditional enemies of Assyria): "I inflicted restlessness on their ghosts *(e-tim-me-shu-nu)*. I deprived them of funerary offerings and pourers of water."[28]

3. *Female "spirits"* (succubi) who cause disease, kill small children, and enter into sexual union with sleeping males. For example, the *ardat lilî* (*"lilû*-woman"; *ardatu* is the usual word for "young woman") was the ghostly sexual partner of unmarried men (presumably she was the explanation for sexual dream-fantasies, nocturnal erections and emissions): "the man whom the *lilû*-woman has chosen"; "*lilû*-woman who has no husband"; "I am the paralyzing *lilû*-woman.[29] In later tradition at least, such sexual union was thought to produce semihuman offspring.[30] The more general designation, *lilîtu*-demon (masculine: *lilû*), describes a malign creature especially dangerous to mothers at childbirth and to infants: "the *lilû*-demons which rage about"; "seizure by the *lilû*-demon"; "the *lilû*-demon should not come near the baby."[31] She seemingly is depicted as a female with the talons of an owl with which she seized her prey.[32] In later oriental demonology she becomes the female demon par excellence, both succubus and slaughterer of children,[33] known as Lilith in Hebrew.

In order to ward off the attack of the various classes of evil spirits, one might resort to *(a)* apotropaic plaques, usually made of clay and showing a picture of the demon and/or the protective deity who was powerful enough to frighten it away;[34] *(b)* apotropaic guardian animals, for example, figurines of magic dogs placed at entrances to the household and engraved with such inscriptions as "Dispatch him!"[35] *(c)* amulets or other charms to be worn on the person, for example, little bronze representations of the demon Pazuzu or strings of yarn which had been knotted in a carefully prescribed way.[36]

Once an evil spirit had actually attacked a person, however, it became necessary to summon expert help, either the magical expert *(āshipu)* who was skilled in incantation or the physician *(asū)* who was skilled in the prescription of drugs.[37] The former, based upon the particular symptoms, tries to isolate the agent and exorcise it. For example, "If his midriff repeatedly blows up, (it is) seizure by a ghost *(eṭemmu)*"; "If he gets severe attacks of pain in his upper face and head...and in the course of days his pubic hairs become thin, it is the hand of *ardat lilī.*"[38] Then follows an incantation, for example,

> (Lamashtu)...has seized (the child) in the abdomen seven times. Remove your claws! Unloose your arms before the wise magic of the hero Ea overtakes you! The door socket is wide for you, the doors are open. Away!...I conjure you by the oath of Ea. May you begone![39]

Sometimes the incantation was part of a larger ritual, as in this direction to the *āshipu:*

> If a man keeps on having fever...you mix frit and bull's dung in the blood of a pig and smear it on the threshold...fill a vessel of six quarts with glowing embers, place it at the head of his bed, encircle his bed with a magic circle of bitter flour...and recite the incantation (entitled) "evil spirits."[40]

The *asū,* on the other hand, generally did not articulate a supernatural cause to disease, and directs his therapy toward the relief of symptoms through prescriptions. For example,

> If a man: on an empty stomach he repeatedly tries to vomit,...his guts are blown up,...he is hot (then) gets cold, and he repeatedly sweats;...this man, severe gastritis (lit. "cramping pains") has struck him; in order to cure him...[41]

The drugs compounded by the *asū* were made from plants, grains, chemicals (e.g., salt), and animal parts, among other ingredients, and were often administered with the recitation of such formulas as "I am physician of the whole land, Lady of Isin, mother who gave birth to the whole land"; "May (the goddess) Gula lay down the charm of life, may the sages apply the bandages!"[42]

What, in Assyro-Babylonian thought, was the origin and purpose of the horde of demons which continually assaulted humans? One perspective is found in the aforementioned Atrahasis Epic. After the gods had fashioned humans to care for the created order, they found that their creatures multiplied rapidly and were creating an uproar.

> Twelve hundred years had not yet passed
> When the land extended and the people multiplied.
> The land was bellowing like a bull.
> The gods got disturbed with their uproar.[43]

Thereupon the gods decree,

Let there be a pestilence (upon mankind).

Humans survive, however, by worshiping the plague-god, and the population continues to increase. Thereupon the gods decide to try other control measures: famine, salinization of the soil, drought, skin irritations. When all of these prove ineffective, the gods resort to a more drastic and potentially total solution: a universal deluge. But even this grand design is thwarted when the god Ea arranged for survivors by means of a great boat. At this point most of the gods are relieved, having come to realize that they will be bereft of their human servants: there will be none to provide them with sacrifices. The god Enlil, however, is furious because of the survivors and is appeased only at the possibility of a new population-control scheme.[44]

(Let there be)...fertile women and barren women;
Let there be among the people a *Pashittu*-demon,
Let it seize the baby from the mother's lap.
Establish the classes of celibate priestesses.
They shall be tabooed, and thus reduce childbearing.

Belief in demons was entirely compatible with the polytheism and dualism of Assyro-Babylonian religion, and would have been suggested by anthropomorphic analogy with human power structures, for example, invading kings or generals surrounded by swarms of henchmen. Furthermore, such demonic forces assisted in the explanation of the harsh realities of Mesopotamian life: destructive floods, repeated invasion and internal strife, fierce summer heat, the infertility of soil, and pestilence.[45]

A demon, unlike a "ghost" *(eṭemmu),* was usually not envisioned as an independent malign force, but served at the bidding of various of the gods and of those who governed the underworld in particular. Thus when Inanna is released from the underworld on condition that a substitute be secured (see above), the presiding gods authorize a detachment of demons to accompany her. Again, when the evil "heptad" *(Sibittu)*[46] want to rampage against the humans above, they must secure the permission of their master Erra. But even he in this instance could not act until the god Marduk, protector of the people of Babylon, is somehow removed from the scene.[47] However, while such "high" gods might often[48] be able to save their people from indiscriminate slaughter, they had no ability to set aside death as the fate of all humans, and not always even to save the worshiper who had offended some divine power, deliberately or inadvertently, and who thus was threatened with premature death. The primary recourse available to a person in the latter situation was to offer sacrifice and prayers of penance to the offended divine power and to trust that one's personal deity will intercede in the divine council.[49]

Fear of such demonic forces was not limited to the Assyro-Babylonians and their predecessors the Sumerians, but is also well attested among the Persians under whose dominion Israel lived during the sixth to the fourth centuries B.C. In their thought, innumerable bodiless demons were ultimately responsible for evil thoughts and deeds among humans, caused "uncleanness" which must be scrupulously removed through lustrations, and often manifested themselves in demon-animals which should be destroyed (e.g., snakes, lizards, and mice). These ubiquitous forces could, however, be held at bay with a variety of apotropaic rites.[50]

Widespread fear of demons is likewise attested among the Canaanites, as evidenced by this seventh-century-B.C. incantation from Arslan Tash in Syria:

> An incantation for the female flying demon.
> . . . . . . . . . . . . . . . . . . . . . . . . . . . . . . . . . . .
> Take these (amulets) and say to the strangling females:
> The house I enter you shall not enter,
> And the courtyard I tread you shall not tread.
> . . . . . . . . . . . . . . . . . . . . . . . . . . . . . . . . . . .
> To the female demon that flies in the darkened room (say):
> Pass by, time and again, O Lilith!
> To the robbing, slaying female (say): Go away![51]

The text has been engraved on a limestone plaque and was apparently meant to be hung in the room where a woman was about to give birth.

Mention may also be made of various apotropaic amulets which archaeologists have recovered from Phoenician (Canaanite) sites.

They show a demon with a wrinkled, bearded face, and animal ears and horns...not unlike the much later depictions of the Christian devil.[52]

Mention has already been made (above) of the apparition (?) which accosted and terrified the Canaanite high-god El, perhaps causing him to wallow in his own excrement and urine.[53]

Finally, there are various Canaanite gods of the underworld, warfare, and pestilence, Resheph foremost among them.[54] He is shown on stelae and plaques in a warlike stance, brandishing an ax over his head and wearing a full quiver of arrows. He is sometimes called "Resheph of the arrow"[55] because like "Apollo the far-shooter" of Greek mythology (cf. *Iliad* 1.45ff.) he was thought to strike mankind with shafts of plague. In addition there is Mot, god of death and drought, whose very name means "death." He and his abode are characterized thusly in the fertility god Baal's instructions to his messengers:

> And descend to the pest house of Earth.
> Be counted with those who descend to Earth.
> Then set face toward his city Oozy,
> Low, the throne of his See,
> Slime, the land of his heritage,
> But beware, O servitors of the gods:
> Do not get close to divine Mot,
> Lest he make you like a lamb in his mouth,
> Like a kid in his gullet's breech you be crushed.[56]

Presumably this description of his realm is patterned after the rock-hewn tombs which characterize the area, into which moisture often seeped.

Demons might attack a person not only because of lack of caution (e.g., failure to wear an amulet or to perform an incantation) or because of some offense to a divine power, but as part of the mischief which a sorcerer might inflict.[57] In such an eventuality it was necessary to recite a prescribed incantation as part of a specific ritual,[58] usually involving the destruction of small images of the sorcerer or sorceress and of those who had hired them. The following incantation, dated about 1000 B.C. and addressed to the sun-god (Shamash), is typical.[59]

Shamash, these are... the images of my sorcerer and sorceress,

. . . . . . . . . . . . . . . . . . . . . . . . . . . . . . . . . . . . . . . . . . . . . . . . . . . . . .

The images of my male and female adversaries,

. . . . . . . . . . . . . . . . . . . . . . . . . . . . . . . . . . . . . . . . . . .

[Upon] me they have laid sorceries, charms, spells, ma[gic]

Hatred, perversion of justice, cutting of the throat, seizure of the mouth,

. . . . . . . . .

An angel of ill, the demon... who sustains evil.

. . . . . . . . . . . . . . . . . . . . . . . . . . . . . . . . . . . . . . . . .

They have bound my mouth, they have taken away my speech

. . . . . . . . . . . . . . . . . . . . . . . . . . . . . . . . . . . . . . . . . . . . . . . . . . . . .

Shamash... these are their images. Since they are not present I am burning their images in the presence of your great divinity.

. . . . . . . . . . . . . . . . . . . . . . . . . . . . . . . . . . . . . . . . . . . . . . . . . . . . .

You are the lord of justice and of right,

. . . . . . . . . . . . . . . . . . . . . . . . . . . . . . . . . . . . .

May their evil sorceries... prostrate them, and attack them and their bodies.

Shamash, let Girru, your associate... destroy them... incinerate them... [pour] out their life like water.

. . . . . . . . . . . . . . . . . . . . . . . . . . . . . . . . . . . . .

Smash them like a pot, let their smoke, as from a furnace, cover [the heavens].

. . . . . . . . . . . .

Let them die, but let me live.

. . . . . . . . . . . . . . . . . . . . . . . .

That I may extoll your greatness and sing your praises...

The ritual description which accompanies the incantation includes the following instructions:

> sweep the ground, sprinkle pure water, set up a table in the presence of Shamash, put on it three food offerings..., set up a censer..., ignite a torch in burning sulphur,... and recite this incantation three times. When they (the images) have been baked, you must quench them in water,... then you must burn them and throw them into a deserted place.... Then the sorceries (will) be resolved.

## C. DESCRIPTION OF THE DEAD AND OF THEIR REALM

### 1. Description of Dead

Since the Assyro-Babylonians believed that humans were fashioned to serve the gods (to till the land, build temples, offer sacrifice), it was logical that they perceive all meaningful existence to be this-worldly. The gods would be interested in their creatures only so long as they were useful, and thus there would be no reason for their having provided for, or for the creatures to expect, a meaningful life after death.

And yet the Assyro-Babylonians (like the Sumerians before them) did not view death as complete annihilation of every aspect of a person: a ghostly image *(eṭemmu)* of the person was thought to survive in the tomb or underworld.[60] It is not so much that the living person possesses an *etemmu* which survives the dissolution of the physical body as that the person at death becomes a fearsome *eṭemmu* which might leave the tomb and terrorize the living. It would be misleading therefore to make comparisons with the later Christian concept of a "soul." (There is, however, a curious passage in the Atrahasis Epic. When the mother-goddess prepares to fashion humans for a work force, she mixes clay with the body of a minor god who has been slain, in order that the *ṭemu*[61] of the god may animate the clay and thus the humans will be *eṭemmu*. Similarly in Enuma Elish it is from the blood of a slain rebellious god that human laborers are fashioned. While these texts do not intend to suggest that humans are in part divine or immortal as would later groups with a similar creation myth,[62] they probably do suggest that life can come only from the gods and belongs intrinsically to them alone.)

Precisely why it was believed that a mere shadow of one's former self continued to subexist is far from clear. It seems to me, however, that one explanation must be regarded with suspicion. That view is expressed by S. G. F. Brandon as follows: "The inability of the ancient Mesopotamians to free themselves from the instinctive belief, present in all primitive peoples, in some form of *postmortem* survival."[63] That such a belief is "instinctive" is of course sheer hypothesis.[64]

We do not have sustained descriptions of the nature of the *eṭemmu,* since texts focus upon their needs and their reaction if neglected. There are, however, occasional fragmentary descriptions, for example, "a ghost, the likeness of a dead man."[65] They seem to have been envisioned as dreamlike apparitions, to judge from the description of Enkidu when he arises from the underworld:

> Scarcely had he opened a hole in the earth,
> When the ghost *(utukku)* of Enkidu, like a gust of wind *(zaqiqu)*,
> Issued forth from the Underworld,
> They embraced and kissed each other.[66]

The dead are sometimes described as semidivine[67] figures:

> The "gods"...have come forth from the grave,
> The evil wind-gusts *(zaqiqu)* have come forth from the grave,
> To demand the payment of rites and the pouring out of libations
> They have come forth from the grave.[68]

Fearsome though such "ghosts" might be, they were sometimes summoned from their abode so that they might be consulted about the future.[69] For example, a letter from the Old Assyrian period (early second millennium B.C.) contains the promise, "We will inquire of the woman oracle-givers and diviners, as well as of the spirits, [whether] [the god] Asshur will continue to care for you," and from the New Assyrian period, "I shall show to the king (a tablet with the prophecy of a *sā'iltu*-necromancer) as follows:...[the spirits] have told me [that he will be] the crown prince of Assyria."[70]

The procedure whereby the "ghosts" were summoned for consultation has only recently become clear.[71] A pit[72] was sunk into the ground to facilitate the ascension of the "ghost," and then tempting offerings of food and drink—blood (needed for revitalization), wine, honey, bread—were placed inside it. Sometimes a miniature ladder was included, presumably to give the "ghost" the right idea. After the consultation had been completed, it was necessary to seal up the hole, lest hordes of the underworld's inhabitants escape to plague the upper world.

This portrait of the deceased, gathered from many sources, is not unlike the shadowy images (*eidōlon,* often translated "shades") of the dead as perceived by the Greeks of the Homeric age. Thus we read in book 11 of the *Odyssey* of Odysseus' attempt to communicate with the deceased poet Teiresias, to whom he has descended in the infernal realm:

> Here Perimedes and Eurylochus held the victims, while I drew my sword and dug the trench a cubit each way. I made a drink offering to all the dead, first with honey and milk, then with wine, and thirdly with water, and I sprinkled white barley meal over the whole, praying

earnestly to the poor feeble ghosts.... When I had prayed sufficiently to the dead, I cut the throats of two sheep and let the blood run into the trench, whereon the ghosts came trooping up... and flitted round the trench with a strange kind of screaming sound that made me turn pale with fear.... I sat where I was with my sword drawn and would not let the poor ghosts come near the blood till Teiresias should have answered my questions.... my mother came up and tasted the blood. Then she knew me at once and spoke fondly to me.[73]

## 2. Description of the Realm of the Dead

The underworld (generally called Aralu) was conceived as a vast city beneath the earth. It is sometimes called "The Great Below," whereas the sky is called "The Great Above" (Inanna's Descent, ll. 1–3). Entrance might be through a crevice in the earth, as when Gilgamesh's musical instruments (?) fall through such an opening;[74] through burial in an underground tomb, since we know that the *etemmu* of the unburied person roamed the land of the living;[75] at the altar of underworld (chthonian) deities, since the altar was located at an entrance to the realm of the particular deity;[76] and apparently beyond the river (ocean) which was thought to surround the world.[77] The realm was thought to be surrounded by seven walls, each with a gate through which the deceased might enter, being divested of their garments by a demon-gatekeeper as they did so (Inanna's Descent, ll. 120–60). Presumably this symbolized the vulnerability and equality of the deceased as they enter this "Land of No Return" (Inanna's Descent, l. 82). Thereafter they entered a realm described as dark (Death of Gilgamesh, l. 26),[78] dusty (Inanna's Descent, l. 44), and "filled with terror" (Vision of the Nether World, rev., l. 13),[79] and were ushered into the presence of the presiding deities. The latter include the goddess of the place, Ereshkigal, and her consort Nergal, god of pestilence and war (the equivalent of the Greco-Roman Mars) and thus responsible for a steady stream of new entrants to his realm;[80] the terrible vizier Namtar, with a body made of composite animal parts, who seizes the entrants with the intent of beheading them (Vision of the Nether World, rev., l. 2); and the seven Anunnaki who serve as judges (Inanna's Descent, ll. 163–66). The basis for judgment is far from clear, if such language is anything more than a vestige of earlier belief. In any case, it was not based upon moral conduct while in the "land of the living" (in contrast to later Persian, Jewish, and Christian ideas). Among the Sumerians, at least, there was the belief that minor figures then guided the entrants to their assigned places.[81] Regular divine visitors included the astral deities, particularly the sun and moon, as they journeyed beneath the earth in their circuit from west to east. A few texts hint that they supplied light on such occasions and also acted as judges[82]—possible background for the later connection between light and judgment (e.g., John 3:19).[83]

## D. EVALUATION

How are we to evaluate the overwhelming number of references to demons and ghosts of the dead which we find in the Assyro-Babylonian literature? Were such beliefs literally held? Or were they more like our modern fairy tales, in which witches, ghosts, and supernatural creatures abound, but which would not necessarily be part of the average person's belief-system? Or are they fossilized language, vestiges of an earlier belief-system which was no longer operative, just as a modern atheist might say "God damn!" and mean nothing more thereby than an expression of anger? When a Canaanite text from Ugarit (fourteenth century B.C.?) reports, "One fifth (of them the plague-god) Resheph gathered to himself," (Keret, I, ll. 18–19) is this anything more than an idiom for "they died of plague"?

At least the following criteria may be used to argue that such belief was taken quite literally:

1. Such malign figures are mentioned not merely in mythological texts (which in any case would have been taken much more seriously then than by modern persons), but in historical chronicles and everyday correspondence.

2. Omen texts and incantations, widely distributed and copied, demand elaborate procedures and time-consuming rituals.

3. Various professionals were available to assist the needy in dealing with the malign forces (e.g., the *šā'iltu*-necromancer and the *āš-ipu*-incantation-priest).

4. Amulets, apotropaic plaques, and images of guardian animals have been widely recovered from ANE excavations.

5. Diviners, including necromancers, were consulted even about important matters of state (e.g., succession to the throne and battle tactics).

6. Tombs have been discovered with tubes *(arūtu)* through which the dead were supplied food and drink.

7. Such offerings could be very expensive, as attested by the mother of the Neo-Babylonian king Nabonidus:

> But I every month without interruption in my finest garments made them a funerary offering of oxen, fat sheep, bread, best beer, wine, sesame oil, honey and all kinds of garden produce, and established abundant offerings of sweet smelling incense as a regular due, and placed it before them.[84]

Or from an Assyrian incantation text:

> "If the 'hand' of the ghost of his father and mother seizes a man... when the spirits *(eṭemmu)* of the dead are mustered, you make a sailboat (and) load it with provisions for them.[85]

My assumption is that such expensive and time-consuming rituals would not have endured if they were mere social conventions devoid of the fear which the literature suggests.

8. Cities contained temples dedicated to the underworld deities, where cultic personnel carried out the established rituals and kept the appropriate festivals. The city of Kutu, for example, was known as a cult center of the Assyro-Babylonian underworld deity Nergal (identified with the Canaanite Resheph and the Greek Mars), concerning whom we have a vast amount of liturgical literature.[86] Such elaborate institutions would not have been formed or supported if they did not meet a pressing need in the everyday life of the population.

# CHAPTER 3

# Death in the Literature of

# the Old Testament

## A. PRELIMINARY CONSIDERATIONS

It will be helpful to begin by articulating the scope, the limitations, and some of the assumptions underlying the following investigation.

1. The focus will not be upon the nature of life after death or upon the historical factors which led to such belief. Such matters have often been treated in the past.[1] Rather, the subject will be the phenomenon of death itself: the emotional reactions to it, and the theological evaluation of it—how it fits into the divine scheme of things.[2] To be sure, this matter cannot be treated in isolation from the doctrine of life after death, insofar as the latter may be a "solution" when death is perceived as incongruous with the divine will for humans.

2. It is the attitudes only of those persons who preserved and shaped the canonical literature which we will seek to recover, that is, the positions which in retrospect are "official" Yahwism. No attempt will be made to recover the much wider "unofficial" range of responses, whether Yahwistic or not.[3]

In the first place, the recovery of the full range of opinion is impossible, given the meager data available to us. To do so we would need specimens of each type of literature which Israel produced, and from every historical period. And even then we would need assume that the literature was an accurate reflection of the culture. In particular one would like to have ordinary correspondence, in hope that it might reflect the everyday attitudes of the people toward death. Furthermore it would be useful to have compositions which focus specifically upon death and the appropriate responses to it. But what we actually have available to us is a highly selective collection of stylized literature, often composite and of uncertain date, very little of which focuses upon death as a phenomenon. (But perhaps the last of these observations is extremely significant and indicative?) And to make matters worse, some of the canonical literature was formulated and/ or preserved by partisan groups which may for a time have reflected a minority opinion.[4] Otherwise put, there may be a gap between "folk religion" and "leading" theologians in any age. In any case, any such "minority" materials as the canon contains were later accepted as "normative" by a wider community.

In the second place, it is only the stances of the canonical literature (as opposed to elements of folk religion) which are regarded as "authoritative" by the believing communities (synagogue and church) in the present. A greater range of Israelite perspectives would be of interest to the modern anthropologist or historian of religion, but less so to those persons who in some fashion regard the Judeo-Christian tradition as important for their own identity. And it is for the latter group that the present volume is primarily intended.

3. The canonical literature contains more than one perspective on death, even after various elements of "unofficial" folk religion are removed. This may be attributed to the fact that the material comes from a period of at least one thousand years, with attendant shifts in perspective in response to cultural contacts and to the shifting fortunes of history.[5] It is therefore difficult to speak accurately of *the* biblical response or perspective (although writers on this topic commonly do so!). To be sure, some responses may predominate and endure longer than others.

There is no reason to expect that shifts or innovations in perspective will be society-wide, as if new ones sounded the death knell of older, traditional ones. On the contrary, religious belief (ancient or modern) is essentially conservative, and older perspectives will continue to be held in some quarters long after the development of newer ones. For example, the Sadducees continued to adhere to the predominant OT stance that the underworld (Sheol) is the final abode of all the dead (who are at most semiconscious), long after the Pharisees (followed by Christianity) accepted the innovative position that there would be a resurrection of the dead.

4. It is not accurate or even helpful, in my opinion, to describe the various shifts or innovations in perspective by using such subjective evaluative terms as "primitive and pessimistic" (for the OT) versus "positive and optimistic" (for the NT), or to speak of "evolution from lower to higher," or of "progressive revelation." For example, one writer has wondered why God allowed "*ignorance* about the condition of man's future existence," by which he seems to mean lack of knowledge of the resurrection of the dead in the early literature of the OT. His conjecture is that "for many centuries it (Israel) was not fit for the reception of a *fuller* and *more intimate* revelation." Only after such deserved calamities as the Babylonian exile was Israel ready "for the sowing of *choicer* seed."[6]

The present work, in contrast, will attempt to present the various perspectives appreciatively. It will see them as attempts to grapple with serious and ongoing issues, and it will not be basically concerned to arrange them in a hierarchical scheme of value.

5. It must be confessed that a modern interpreter likely cannot do full justice to any ancient perspective, biblical or otherwise. Because of the vast cultural and linguistic gap which separates the Bible from our world,[7] we cannot understand or appreciate any ancient situation or belief as an on-the-spot observer would. The necessary background data (political, social, economic, psychological, religious) is simply not available to us. Thus an element of humility is certainly in order as we undertake the following investigation.

6. Secondary literature on this topic will present the reader with a bewildering and sometimes contradictory array of approaches, emphases, and conclusions. This is caused in part by the innate difficulty of the materials (some of which have been mentioned above) but also by the questionable methodologies and assumptions which some modern writers have brought to the task. A random sampling follows.

a. One may find differing opinions on the most basic of issues. For example, ancient Israelites may be described as evidencing little anxiety about death,[8] or as regarding it with complete horror.[9] Immortality and resurrection may be described as very late doctrines, appearing only at the end of the OT period,[10] or based upon comparative Ugaritic lexicography, they may be posited over a wide era of the ANE as far back as the second millennium B.C.[11]

b. One may read that "on the whole, it can be said of the biblical writings that they have no theology of death or of an afterlife,"[12] and at the same time find extended treatment of the subject! But while it is true that the Bible is often silent about many aspects of Israelite thought on this dimension of human existence, such silence could within itself be taken as evidence of a profound theological position.

c. Very often the diversity of biblical perceptions of death (as a mode or realm of existence, as a power, as biological cessation) and the range of its reactions to it (as a natural expectation or as an enemy) will be ignored or masked behind a monolithic description of *the* biblical view. In such descriptions it is usually a NT perspective (death as the "enemy") which has been projected onto the entirety of the canon.[13]

d. Sometimes authors will indulge in questionable and in any case unnecessary Christian and denominational apologetics. For example, Israel's preprophetic thought may be described as characterized by "defects" and "heathen survivals" with Yahweh depicted therein as a narrow, nationalistic war-god who has no control over the underworld (Sheol). By contrast, prophetic thought may be described as monotheistic, wherein Yahweh's power was extended not only to the entire world but to the realm of the dead, and thereby "the way is prepared for the coming of Christianity."[14] Such an evolutionary scheme, reflecting the zeitgeist of the late nineteenth and early twentieth centuries, is no longer characteristic of biblical scholarship.

e. On the one hand one may read that early Israelite and even Yahwistic perceptions of the dead are in strong contrast to those of her neighbors.[15] On the other hand one may encounter massive use of ANE parallels (and even Indo-European models) in order to clarify Israelite belief or even to indicate basic similarity.[16]

f. Persons who read widely in this area will be confronted with a bewildering phalanx of terminology: future life, life after death, resurrection, bodily assumption, intermediate state, immortality, eternal life. The meaning intended by the terms may vary from one author to the next. A given author may use several of the terms interchangeably, or sometimes with various shades of distinction. For example, resurrection of the body may be viewed as a form of immortality[17] or as its antithesis.[18] And the troublesome term *immortality* may be used in at least the following senses:[19]

1. As a quality intrinsic only to divine beings which distinguishes them from humans: "Not everything is within man's reach, for the human race is not immortal" (Ecclus. 17:30); God "who alone has immortality" (1 Tim. 6:16).[20] The same sentiment seems to be expressed in Mesopotamian thought: "When the gods created mankind, they allotted death to him, retaining life in their own hands."[21] However, in mythological texts, minor gods can be slain by more powerful ones, as can older generations by their offspring.[22]

2. As deathlessness which the gods may exceptionally convey to deserving human beings, or as a postdeath continuation of meaningful existence which they may routinely convey to their faithful worshipers. The former condition is claimed by the Babylonian flood hero,[23] it is promised to the young man Aqhat by the goddess Anat,[24] and it seems to have been accorded to a few persons in the OT.[25] The latter expectation seems to have characterized much of late Judaism and also Christianity, where it may or may not involve a resurrection of the body.[26]

3. As an intrinsic quality of human beings. They possess a "soul" naturally akin to the divine, ingenerate and incorruptible, which exists for a time in a mortal and vulnerable body. Such a view is found in certain of the Greek philosophers, among the Hellenistic "mystery religions," and among the Gnostics of the NT period.[27] When St. Paul[28] and the early fathers of the church[29] use the term *immortality,* they usually try to distinguish it from this basically Greek usage by insisting that it is a gift of the deity.

4. As a characterization of the phantomlike remnant of the person which early Greeks (Homer) and Israelites thought inhabited the tomb or the underworld. While most scholars have tended to describe such a status of the dead as near-annihilation, subexistence, or meaninglessness (especially as it is described in the OT), it has nonetheless a minimal continuity with earthly existence.[30]

5. For the legacy one leaves behind, whereby one may be remem-

bered. Thus the Israelites treasured offspring and reputation;[31] Gilgamesh, king of Uruk, reflecting upon the possibility of death in battle, remarks, "Should I fall, I shall have made me a name: 'Gilgamesh,' they will say, 'against the fierce (monster) Huwawa has fallen!'";[32] and the Spartan poet Tyrtaeus speaks of the valiant soldier who is slain in battle: "His glory or his name shall never die; though 'neath the ground, he deathless shall remain."[33]

## B. DEMONS

Since Israel was surrounded by peoples for whom the existence of demons was a self-evident reality and for whom the use of apotropaic amulets and the recitation of incantations was a constant necessity (see chap. 2), it is only to be expected that her population would share such belief and practice. It is therefore surprising that in her canonical literature demons are either ignored as irrelevant, considered to be Yahweh's agents, reduced to common nouns (demythologized, desacralized) or to powers of nature, or are treated as intrusions from neighboring cults and thus condemned.[34]

The predominant reason for this banishing of demons lies in Israel's unique monotheistic[35] covenant theology. Yahweh simply dispossesses the other divine powers from their realm of activity. It is Yahweh who causes sickness and brings health:

> There is no god beside me; I kill and make alive;[36] I wound and I heal.
> (Deut. 32:39)

It is Yahweh who controls the fertility which some attribute to Baal:

> She (Israel) did not know that it was I who gave her the grain, the wine, and the oil.
> (Hos. 2:8 [Hebrew, 10])

It was Yahweh alone who delivered his people from bondage:

> The Lord alone did lead him, and there was no foreign god with him.
> (Deut. 32:12)

It is Yahweh alone who controls death:

> Thou turnest man back to dust...
> (Ps. 90:3)

Indeed, the Second Isaiah can sing amidst the captives in Babylon:

> I am the Lord, who made all things,
> who stretched out the heavens alone,
> who spread out the earth—who was with me?
>                    (44:24)

> Before me no god was formed,
> nor shall there be any after me.
> I, I am the Lord
> and beside me there is no savior.
>                    (43:10–11)

Thus the entirety of Israel's gratitude and attention is focused upon Yahweh. There is simply no room, indeed no need, to acknowledge the existence of the demonic.[37]

That demons may have been worshiped in ancient Israel is suggested by such physical evidence as an amulet from a seventh-century-B.C. occupation level at Achzib,[38] showing a bearded, horned demon. (To be precise, however, we have no way of knowing whether it belongs to an Israelite or to some other ethnic group who resided at the site, whether it was used to ward off demons or was a mere curio.) In addition, the biblical text itself directly attests instances when individuals or groups in Israel indulged in such religious belief and practice. Among the most common types of demons are the following.

1. *Shedim,*[39] a term which seems related to the Assyro-Babylonian *Shedu.* (The latter were sometimes thought to act as protective spirits, but at other times were thought to be malign.) Thus the Book of Deuteronomy complains:

> They (Israel) sacrificed to demons which were
>     no gods, to gods they had never known,
> to new gods that had come in of late,
>     whom your fathers had never dreaded.
>                    (32:17)

2. *Śe'irim,*[40] apparently thought to resemble the hairy satyrs of the Greeks. (The related word *śe'ir* means "he-goat.") They may have been considered to be genii of fertility, and sacrifices were sometimes offered to them. Like the demons of the Assyro-Babylonians, they seem to have been especially fond of lurking in ruins (Isa. 34:14).

> So they shall no more slay their sacrifices for satyrs, after whom they
> play the harlot.
>
> (Lev. 17:7)

It should be noted that the worship of such creatures is usually
described as characteristic only of specific groups within Israel, and
only at specific periods. The texts just quoted clearly express the
opinion that such practice was in opposition to Yahwism. And thus
various reforms included attacks upon their institutions; for example, 2 Kings 23:8 apparently reports that the high places (altars)
of the satyrs[41] were destroyed at the time of Josiah.

In addition to these overt references to limited and condemned
worship of demons, there are other references that cannot be taken
so literally.

1. Instances where demonic figures seemingly have been reduced
to agents at Yahweh's bidding. They have been denied an autonomy of their own, removed from a polytheistic environment and
made part and parcel of Yahwism. They are now indistinguishable
from the will of Israel's God.

> God came from Teman.... His glory covered the heavens.... Before
> him goes Deber; Resheph follows at his heels.
>
> (Hab. 3:3–5, trans. mine)

Resheph is a well-attested Canaanite plague-demon.[42] The typol-
ogy here seems to be that of the divine warrior who is accompanied
into battle by his troops.[43] It could be argued, however, that the depolytheizing had proceeded even further and that the words *deber*
and *resheph* are here treated like common nouns. Thus the RSV
merely reads "pestilence and plague." Fulco prefers to see depictions
of "lesser divinity."[44]

2. Instances where the demythologizing clearly has been total: the
demons have been reduced to a designation for the distress which
they were thought to cause. Their "names" are now nothing more
than common nouns.[45]

> (In Zion, God) broke the *rshpy-qsht*, the shield, the sword, and the
> weapons of war.
>
> (Ps. 76:3 [Hebrew, 4])

*Rshpy-qsht* is obviously a military implement in a list of such common nouns. The RSV translates it as "the flaming arrow."[46] Literally it is "the reshephs of the bow," seemingly a reference to the military power of the god Resheph.

Or again, the malign *Sibittu* (the Seven), so feared in Mesopotamian incantations and invoked in terrible treaty-curses, survive but as sevenfold enumerations of the punishment which Yahweh visits upon those who disobey him.

> The Lord will smite you with consumption, and with fever, inflammation, and fiery heat, and with drought, and with blasting, and with mildew.... The Lord will cause you to be defeated before your enemies; you shall ... flee seven ways before them.
>
> (Deut. 28:22, 25)

When Job describes the inevitability of human trouble, he uses an idiom which in Canaanite thought would have referred to the winged companions of the god Resheph.[47]

> Man indeed is born for trouble and
> The Sons of Resheph circle overhead.
>
> (5:7, trans. mine)

References to demons are more frequent in the Psalms, for example,

> You shall not fear the terror of the night,
> nor the arrow that flies by day,
> nor the pestilence *(deber)* that stalks in darkness,
> nor the destruction that wastes at noonday.
>
> (91:5-6)

Since many of the psalms are very ancient, some with possible parallels to Canaanite hymns, and since liturgical language tends to be conservative (cf. modern "thou" in prayers), we need not be surprised that such language is more frequent in them. Therefore we need not automatically see it as indicative of living Israelite belief. In any case, *even if* the formulators of such psalms and those who recited them at whatever stage of Israel's history had understood the language quite literally to refer to demons, it must be noted that little fear of them is evidenced. God is sufficient to insure the safety of his people.

There are a number of practices or customs in the OT which may well have their origin in apotropaic measures against demons but which, when demons ceased to be considered as vital forces, nonetheless continued to be observed. Among them are bells on the robe of the high priest (Exod. 28:33–35), blue coloration of garments (Num. 15:38), verses of Scripture deposited in the doorposts (Deut. 6:8; 11:18), the use of incense (Lev. 16:12–13).[48] Perhaps also to be included are the purificatory sin offering (Lev. 4:4–12), ritual contamination (Lev. 6:24–30), and the period of impurity associated with childbirth (Lev. 12).[49]

The fact that the neighboring peoples continued to acknowledge the existence of demons, as did elements within the land of Israel, set the stage for the reemergence of the demonic powers at a later period within the history of the canonical literature. This reemergence found its opportunity during the postexilic period when historical events seem to challenge the salvation-history in a most radical fashion. (See below and chaps. 4–6.)

## C. A CULT OF THE DEAD?

Since a cult of dead ancestors and the attendant practice of necromancy is so well attested throughout the ANE, not only among Semites (chap. 2) but among the Greeks and Romans,[50] we could assume even without the slightest evidence that it was known and practiced in ancient Israel as well.

That necromancy (the oracular consultation of the dead) was practiced is clear first of all from the narrative account in 1 Samuel 28. King Saul, trying to estimate how his battle with the Philistines will turn out, has found that the usual channels of communication with the divine realm (dreams, *urim*,[51] and prophets) have all failed. Thereupon he resorts to necromancers, having previously banished them ("wizards and mediums," v. 3) from his realm. Since one of them is still resident at the city of Endor, he journeys there during the night to consult her. She apparently follows a procedure that is well known to us from other ANE texts, including digging a hole[52] in the crust of the earth so that the dead may ascend for questioning. She then announces that the "divine"[53] deceased prophet Samuel is now present, and describes him as "an old man...wrapped in a robe" (v. 13). A conversation between Saul and Samuel is then reported, ending with the latter's statement that Saul will lose his life in battle the next day.

Although one scholar has argued that this story indicates a canonical belief in the efficaciousness of the necromancer's art,[54] it must be pointed out that the purpose of the story is not to attest or deny its effectiveness but to relate another tragic episode in the decline of King Saul, which includes mental deterioration: he resorts to the very practice which he has previously outlawed, only to have it backfire in his face. Not only does Samuel chide him for "disturbing me by bringing me up" (v. 15), but he announces that Saul is worthy of death because of his previous disobedience (v. 18)—to which, he might have said, could now be added a violation of the prohibition against consulting necromancers! It is not at all clear to me, therefore, just how seriously the formulators and preservers of this story took the "efficaciousness" of necromancy.

Modern "spiritualists" sometimes cite this text as evidence that the Bible teaches that the dead continued to survive and could be contacted for oracles, and thus that such modern practice is compatible with Judeo-Christianity. However, at least the following cautions are in order: whether or not the witch was a Yahwist, or even an Israelite, we are not told; Saul himself apparently does not see Samuel arise from the earth, but relies rather upon the affirmation of the medium that this has happened; and the alleged conversation is likely through the medium rather than directly with Samuel—perhaps one should say, *with* the medium.[55] And even to grant this much is to presuppose the essential historicity of the account! In any case, Saul hears a reaffirmation of that which he already knows: God has rejected him in favor of David (v. 17; cf. 15:23–28). H. W. Wolff rightly remarks concerning the episode that

> in its very success it strikingly demonstrates the absurdity of the undertaking....Thus this story of the conjuring up of the dead, which is unique in the Old Testament, shows that nothing is to be expected from the spirits of the dead beyond what has been witnessed to by living messengers. On exactly the same lines, Dives' request is rejected in Jesus' parable...(Luke 16:27f.).[56]

What we would not expect, given the wide evidence for necromancy in the ANE, is the strong rejection of it which we find in the OT. The following is a sampling of the prohibitions:

> If a person turns to mediums and wizards, playing the harlot after them, I...will cut him off from among his people.
>
> (Lev. 20:6)

> A man or a woman who is a medium or a wizard shall be put to death; they shall be stoned with stones, their blood shall be upon them.
>
> (Lev. 20:27)

> When you come to the land which the Lord your God gives you.... There shall not be found among you...a medium, or a wizard, or a necromancer.
>
> (Deut. 18:9, 11)

> And when they say to you, "Consult the mediums and the wizards who chirp and mutter," should not a people consult their God? Should they consult the dead on behalf of the living?
>
> (Isa. 8:19)

While it has been argued that such prohibitions refer only to foreign cults and to foreign families who indulge in their ancestral rites,[57] it seems preferable to me to take the texts at face value: as absolute prohibitions. There is no indication in the text itself that such a distinction is being made. But what would be the basis for such vehement opposition? (1) Is it merely part of Israel's well-known aversion to Canaanite ways of doing things, that is, a suspicion of things foreign?[58] Note how various prohibited practices in Leviticus 20, including necromancy, are described as "customs of the nation which I am casting out before you" (v. 23). (2) Or is it that necromancy is a mere "superstition"[59] which the biblical theologians want Israel to transcend, that is, the dead have no knowledge of the living and their future, such that the entire enterprise is futile? Certainly a number of biblical texts assert that the dead have no such ability: for example, "The living know at least that they will die, the dead know nothing;...nor will they ever again take part in whatever is done under the sun...there is neither achievement, nor planning, nor knowledge, nor wisdom in Sheol where you are going" (Eccles. 9:5-6, 10, *JB*). Such a perspective, if widely held,[60] would certainly seem to negate a belief in the efficacy of necromancy! (3) Or is it that necromancy, like magic, was viewed as part of secular knowledge, "which seduces man into arrogant self-sufficiency,"[61] as when Saul, having failed to get a response from Yahweh, assumes that he can secure reliable information from another source (1 Sam. 28)? Note that Isaiah, in the passage quoted above, chides the people for consulting mediums rather than God. Whatever the original reason(s), they are not articulated in the text in connection with the prohibitions themselves, and more than one motivation may have been subsequently operative. And it may be that with the passage of time, the knowledge and ability which the dead were perceived to have were significantly reduced, such that efficaciousness, if attributed to necromancy in the early period, had eroded away by the postexilic period (e.g., in Ecclesiastes and Job).

When we turn from necromancy to the rites performed for the dead, Israel's (canonical) attitude becomes clearer. No funeral rites are prescribed, but a great many were carried out, as we learn from narrative literature (e.g., rending of clothes, fasting, and covering the lip).[62] A few actions are prohibited, presumably because of their association with foreign cults: for example, cutting or marking the flesh (Lev. 19:28), shaving the forehead (Deut. 14:1). Contact with a corpse or a tomb made one ineligible to participate in the cult of Yahweh (i.e., it rendered one ritually "unclean") until a time-consuming ritual had been performed (Num. 5:2; 19:1–22). A priest could make such contact only in the case of the nearest kin (Lev. 21:1–4) and the chief priest could not make such contact at all (Lev. 21:10–12). Such "impurity" may have had its origin in fear of a death-demon (still thought to lurk in the corpse)[63] or in a rejection of the divinization of the dead in the ancestor-cult. All such powers are now denied existence, and a rigid line is drawn between the dead and the cultic sphere of Yahweh. To the extent that rites are performed for the dead, they have been robbed of religious significance and reduced to custom, that is, to human expression of grief or sympathy.[64] Even mummification, connected by the Egyptians with the cult of Osiris, can be performed on the bodies of Jacob and Joseph (Gen. 50:2, 26) without religious implication.

Not only do the dead not reside in a demonic realm, they are not able to roam the earth and terrorize the living even if offerings of food and drink are not made to them.[65] Yahweh's demand that worship and gratitude be directed exclusively to him in whose hands Israel's past, present, and future lay was incompatible with the idea that the dead could in any way affect the fate of the living. One was thus freed from a preoccupation with death: freed from time-consuming incantations and freed from the economic burdens which the ancestor-cult of the neighbors imposed.[66]

## D. FOLK EXPLANATIONS OF THE ORIGIN OF DEATH

Israel's canonical understanding of death within the larger scheme of things, that is, how it relates to the will of the deity, is found in the Genesis creation accounts. Behind the present account in chapters 2–3 there may be two earlier folk explanations (etiologies)[67] of human mortality.[68]

1. A protohuman couple in primeval time was warned by its creator not to partake of the fruit of "the tree of knowledge": "when you eat of it you will surely die" (2:17). This may suggest that the couple was created to be immortal and that they might have remained so. However, as the result of *hubris* that leads to disobedience, they are expelled from their paradise home, condemned to toil and pain, and told that they will "return to the ground" from which they were created (3:19). Death would thus be an intrusion into the Creator's design, a curse under which humans were of necessity placed, a manifestation of their "fallen" state. What would have given rise to such an "explanation" for mortality? Does it reflect the very *hubris* which it decries: unable to accept mortality as fitting for humans, the storyteller proposed that we were intended for immortality but relinquished it through our own actions? Or does the basis for the "explanation" lie in analogy with other human activity and failure: is it an extrapolation from the fate of the unsuccessful political usurper who is put to death by his master? This is a rather common theme in OT literature (e.g., Ezek. 28).[69]

2. The protohuman couple was designed by the Creator to be mortal. "The man" (Hebrew *ha-'adam*)[70] was fashioned from the ground *(ha-'adamah):*

And the Lord God fashioned "the man,"
(of) clay[71] from the ground (he fashioned him).
(2:7, trans. mine)

Presumably mortality was intended for this creature, just as it was
for all of the others which the deity likewise fashioned from the
ground:

So out of the ground *(ha-'adamah)* the Lord God formed every beast of
the field and every bird of the air.

(2:19, cf. Eccles. 3:19–20)

Life results when the deity forces breath *(neshamah)* into "the
man," and he becomes a "living creature" (2:7, *NEB*). Presumably
the same procedure, in the understanding of the Genesis storyteller,
would have been followed in the case of the other animals: God forced
"breath" into them,[72] although this is not specifically related since the
story focuses upon the humans. In any case, the other animals are
called by the same designation, "living creatures" (1:20, 24).[73] All
have the same divinely given life-force (breath) within them:

When you hide your face, they (all animals) are stricken;
When you take away their breath *(ruaḥ),* they gasp and return to their
clay.
When you send your breath *(ruaḥ),* they are created (anew?).

(Ps. 104:29, trans. N. Tromp)

It is only to be expected, then, that humans be forbidden access to
a source of rejuvenation (or immortality?): a "tree of life" which
grows in the midst of their garden paradise.

Then the Lord God said, "... lest he (humankind) put forth his hand
and take also from the tree of life, and eat, and live for ever"—

(3:22)

At this point the text breaks off, creating the impression that this
folk explanation has been only partially preserved. In any case, the
humans will remain as they were created: mortal.

... until you return to the ground,
for out of it you were taken;
you are clay,
and to clay you shall return.
(3:19, trans. mine)

To be sure, this explanation has been merged with the one previously discussed, so that as the entire chapter now stands, the statement about returning to dust appears to be punishment, to be a fate not intended for the humans.

It must be stressed, however, that the material in Genesis 2—3 can be read as a continuous story rather than as a combination of two earlier and conflicting folk accounts:[74] the couple is continually rejuvenated by eating from the "tree of life." However, because of their disobedience in eating from the "tree of knowledge," they are expelled from the garden, lose access to the "tree of life," and thus remain as they were created: mortals. Nonetheless, later generations would have different interpretations of the story, along the lines of the two previously suggested folk explanations. Etiology (or interpretation-possibility) number 1 (death as punishment) had no influence upon subsequent OT literature,[75] although there is the related idea that human sin leads to *premature* death. Likewise, the idea of death as punishment played very little role in Rabbinic literature,[76] although there are occasional statements such as "There is no death without sin" (TB Shab. 55a). By contrast, this etiology has played a central role in Christian theology, which seems anticipated in the Wisdom of Solomon (second century B.C.): "Do not invite death by the error of your life...because God did not make death" (1:13); "God created man for immortality...it was the devil's spite that brought death into the world" (2:23-24, *NEB*).[77] Since death, in this view, was not a part of the Creator's original design but rather came about within what could be viewed as "history,"[78] perhaps death could be abolished if sinful human nature could be overcome. Thus St. Paul is able to suggest, in view of his interpretation of Jesus as the Christ, "Freed from the commands of sin,...the end is eternal life. For sin pays a wage, and the wage is death" (Rom. 6:22-23, *NEB*).

Etiology (or interpretation-possibility) number 2 (mortality as the Creator's design for humans) seems to be the basic perspective of the OT literature (as we will discuss in detail below). It is also the basic perspective of the Rabbinic literature, for example, of Rabbi Meir, who remarks that the description of creation in Genesis 1 as "good" includes the phenomenon of death (Genesis Rabbah 9:5). Other rabbis remark that the angel of death was created on the very first day

(Tanhuma, Va-Yeshev 4), that is, that death was part of God's design for humans; or that the unique absence of the description "good" for the second day of creation indicates that the underworld was created then, that is, death was anticipated as part of the world design.

The Genesis etiologies (or etiology) seem to preserve a faint echo of tablet XI of the Gilgamesh Epic (part of which we discussed in the previous chapter). The hero, Gilgamesh, has been told that humans were created to be mortal: "When the gods created mankind, death they ordained for him, retaining life for themselves." This is of course the message of Genesis etiology 2, and Gilgamesh laments that it is an accurate appraisal of the human situation. He then seeks advice from the one person said to have escaped death: the Babylonian equivalent of Noah, hero of the universal-flood story. This person, however, had been given a special dispensation by the gods and thus can be of no help to Gilgamesh. He does, however, suggest a magic plant which if eaten will restore (temporarily) one's youth. Gilgamesh finds the plant only to have it eaten by a serpent, who then sheds its skin and appears to be reborn. The story thus contains an etiology on the seeming longevity of snakes and indirectly on the mortality of humans. The Genesis material transforms the serpent into something approximating the human ego: rather than stealing a magic plant, the serpent goads the couple into rebellion against the creator's guidelines. Thereupon they are forbidden access to the magic tree. The etiological theme, as it relates to the serpent, does not stress its longevity but the resultant hostility between its descendants and those of the couple: "I will put enmity between you and the woman, between your brood and hers" (3:15, *NEB*).

## E. MANIFESTATIONS OF "DEATH"

The term *death* is used in the literature of the OT in at least three senses: (1) as a metaphor for those things which detract from life as Yahweh intends it, among them illness, persecution, despair, and nonparticipation in the life of the covenant community; (2) as a "power" in opposition to the created order; (3) for biological cessation, usually in the sense of the end of a given individual's historical existence, and less frequently as the inevitable fate of all humans. It is the last of these usages—that is, Israel's emotional reactions to and theological reflections upon mortality—which will be our primary concern in the pages which follow. But the other two must be discussed, and that primarily for two reasons: *(a)* modern writers sometimes confuse the usages,[79] and *(b)* the first and third usages are derived ultimately from the second: a malign power brings misfortune and death. It is part of the triumph of Yahwism over older conceptions that the connection between the usages is broken. During the Intertestamental period, however, a holistic perception will begin to reemerge (chap. 5).

## 1. Death as metaphor

> The Lord kills and brings to life;
>> he brings down to Sheol (the underworld) and raises up.
> The Lord makes poor and makes rich;
>> he brings low, he also exalts.
>
> (1 Sam. 2:6–7)

The text deals with Yahweh's total control over the destiny of humans: he has the power to abase and to establish. To "kill" and to "give life" are said entirely in relation to this-worldly fortunes, with no suggestion that biological cessation or recovery (resurrection) is meant. Sheol, as often in the OT, is likewise a metaphor (common noun)[80] for misfortunes of various sorts, as when the prophet Jonah, depicted as praying from the digestive system of a great fish, says: "I went down to the Land (underworld)[81] whose (door-)bars closed behind me forever; yet you brought up my life from the Pit,[82] O Lord my God" (2:6, trans. mine).

> Consider and answer me, O Lord my God;
>> lighten my eyes, lest I sleep the sleep of death;
> lest my enemy say, "I have prevailed over him";
>> lest my foes rejoice because I am shaken.
>
> (Ps. 13:3–4)

One may note the seemingly parallel notion: being routed by one's earthly enemies and experiencing "death." One might cite, as an ANE parallel, the Hittite king who announces that he has killed his enemy and chased him out of the country![83]

"Death," then, tends to be used to describe the various conditions which detract from the full potential which Yahweh intended for his creatures; it is used as a value judgment on the quality of life, so that a weak and ineffective person, a "nobody," can be called a "dead dog" (1 Sam. 24:14). On the other hand, "life" is more than biological functioning: it is life to the full, as Yahweh intended it.[84]

> See, I have set before you this day life and good, death and evil... I have set before you life and death, blessing and curse; therefore choose life.
>
> (Deut. 30:15, 19)

The text goes on to point out that by choosing life (equated with the "good"), one may secure (biologically long) life.

There is of course a connection between this metaphoric usage and the biological usage. Biological death could be viewed as a weakening of the life-force,[85] just as psychological, social, and religious death (the despair, alienation, and doubt of the psalmist) are a diminution of the vitality and possibility which God wills for his people. Curiously, the focus of Israel's canonical literature is usually upon metaphoric "death." Anxiety has been largely concentrated upon the psychological and social modes rather than upon the biological one. (One may wonder if we should speak of "concentration" or of [evasive?] "transferal.")

## 2. Death as a Power

While this seems well attested among Israel's neighbors (in the form of chthonian deities, demons, and malign "ghosts" of the deceased: see chap. 2), Israel itself has largely transformed such forces into minor figures at Yahweh's bidding or to mere proper names (see sec. B above).[86] For example, when one of Job's friends describes deterioration of the body, he uses a formalized idiom: "The firstborn of death consumes his limbs" (18:13). He likely would not mean thereby what a Canaanite might mean, that the god Mot ("Death"), a demonic, autonomous power,[87] had seized the person.

Again, there is a connection between this vestigial usage and the other two: illness, persecution, and so forth may once have been called "death" because they were regarded as manifestations of the power of divine Mot, as was biological cessation itself.

## 3. Biological Death

**a.** *Anthropology.* Human beings, as depicted in Israel's canonical creation stories (Genesis 2–3), are not complex creatures who are composed of a number of constituent elements. Such concepts as body, soul, and spirit, familiar to us from later anthropologies, are entirely alien to the stories. Rather, humans are depicted as claylike flesh that has been animated by a life-force which has its origin in the divine realm. It would be improper to say that in such a view a person *has* a body, as if "person" were more elemental, a possessor. Rather, one *is* a body, animated.

> And the Lord God fashioned "the man" *(ha-'adam)*, (of) clay from the
>    ground *(ha-'adamah)* (he fashioned him);
> and he breathed into his nostrils the breath of life *(nishmat-hayyim)*,
> and "the man" became a living creature *(nephesh hayyah)*.
>                                                              (Gen. 2:7, trans. mine)

> You make man return to dust,
>    and say, "Return, O mortals!"
>       (Ps. 90:3, trans. mine)

> Remember that you make me like a vase;
>    and will you make me return to clay (now)?
>       (Job 10:9, trans. N. Tromp)

The image is that of a potter who fashions a fragile object from ceramic clay.[88] What would have given rise to such an image, likewise attested in other ANE stories?[89] Perhaps it was suggested to the storyteller by the observation that human flesh is often reddish in color, like iron-rich soil. Note the connection made between the place-name Edom (lit. "Red [Region]") and Esau, the ruddy-skinned ancestor of the Edomites (Gen. 25:25). Furthermore, there was the observation that the human body, when placed in the underground tomb, seemed to deteriorate and merge (back?) into the soil. And as a bonus, such a folk explanation made possible the kind of pun in which Semites seemed to delight: *'adam/'adamah,* let the creature be called "adam" because he is "adamic."[90] It is important to realize, however, that behind the imagery of the folk explanation and behind the pun lies the basic point: the radical distinction between the creator and the created.

This holistic, "earthy" creature is animated by a life-force *(neshamah;* more usually elsewhere, *nephesh* or *ruah)* which belongs intrinsically to God[91] and which resides in the blood and/or in the breath.[92] Such loci are hardly surprising, given the fact that breathing is universally regarded as a "vital" sign and that loss of blood leads to weakness and eventual death, at which point the blood ceases to flow.

You shall not eat flesh with its life *(nephesh)*, that is, its blood.

(Gen. 9:4)

If any man of the house of Israel...eats any blood, I will set my face against that person.... For the life *(nephesh)* of the flesh is in the blood.

(Lev. 17:10–11)

But the eyes of the wicked will fail;
all way of escape will be lost to them,
and their hope is to breathe their last (lit. "to breathe out their *nephesh*").

(Job 11:20)

His (the monster Leviathan's)[93] breath *(nephesh)* kindles coals,
and a flame comes forth from his mouth.

(Job 41:21; Heb. v. 13)

These two loci of the vital (life-)force, both here expressed by the single term *nephesh*, may be related as follows: *nephesh*, apparently originally meaning "throat,"[94] came to mean secondarily *(a)* "breath" (which passes through the throat) and *(b)* "life," whose presence is signaled both by breathing and flow of blood.[95]

If he (God) should take back to himself his wind *(ruah)*,
gather to himself his breath *(neshamah)*,
all flesh would perish together,
and humans would return to clay.

(Job 34:14–15, trans. mine)

I will bring a flood...to destroy all flesh in which is the breath of life *(ruah hayyim)*.

(Gen. 6:17)

*Nephesh* and *ruah* therefore are not separate, elemental components of humans (the "soul" and "spirit" of later anthropology; cf. the "dichotomy" and "trichotomy" of R. H. Charles's analysis),[96] but are manifestations of vitality (sometimes interchangeable and sometimes slightly distinguishable). In the words of Wolff, "We can see here the stereometry of synthetic thinking, which approaches a phenomenon from different sides."[97]

Another meaning that *nephesh* comes to have is "(living) creature": person, individual.

Whoever (lit. "Any *nephesh* who") does any work on this same day, that person *(nephesh)* I will destroy from among his people.

(Lev. 23:30)

Thus we read both of "living creature" (*nephesh hayyah,* Gen. 2:7) and "deceased creature," that is, "corpse" (*nephesh mēth,* Num. 6:6). The latter idiom has been misunderstood by some modern interpreters to mean "a dead soul" (i.e., some constituent part of humans which, like the body, can die)[98] or a death-demon (lit. "force of death").[99] Such interpretations are countered by other texts which more clearly define Israelite anthropology and by the parallel grammatical construction *nephesh hayyah.* In conclusion, some texts will describe the human *as* nephesh, while others will treat the human as a *possessor* of nephesh.

b. *The "Mechanics" of Death.* Biological death results when the life-force ceases to animate the flesh. The biblical idiom usually involves the idea of "going out":

> And as her life-force *(nephesh)* was going out,[100] because she was dying...
>
> (Gen. 35:18, trans. mine)

> ...as they faint like wounded men
>    in the streets of the city,
> as their life *(nephesh)* is poured out
>    on their mothers' bosom.
>
> (Lam. 2:12)

> When his breath *(ruaḥ)* departs,[101]
> he returns to his earth *('adamah).*
>
> (Ps. 146:4)

Since the life-force comes from God, it was only natural to associate its departure with his will (thereby depolytheizing death):

> His illness was so severe that there was no breath *(neshamah)* left in him.... Then he (Elijah) stretched himself upon the child three times and cried to the Lord, "O Lord my God, let this child's life-force *(nephesh)* come into him again.
>
> (1 Kings 17:17, trans. mine)

> (And Elijah said,) "It is enough; now, O Lord, take away my life *(nephesh).*"
>
> (1 Kings 19:4)

> When you take away their breath *(ruaḥ),* they gasp and return to their clay.
>
> (Ps. 104:29, trans. N. Tromp)

What is the fate of the life-force upon its departure from creatures, human or otherwise? A few passages speak of its return to
God:

> If he (God) should take back to himself his wind *(ruaḥ)*,
>    gather to himself his breath *(neshamah)* ...
>                              (Job 34:14, trans. mine)

> The clay returns to the earth as it was,
> and the breath *(ruaḥ)*[102] returns to God who gave it.
>                              (Eccles. 12:7, trans. mine)

There is no hint, in this idea of a "return to God," of the later concept of a "soul" which includes memory and personality. Rather,
the life-force, whether conceived in terms of blood or breath, is an
impersonal energy which belongs intrinsically only to God and
which dissipates at death. Indeed, it is only in the relatively late
book of Ecclesiastes that we find raised a question of the distinctiveness of the human *ruaḥ*—a question which the author answers in a
skeptical-to-negative mode:

> For the fate of the sons of men and the fate of the beasts is the same: as
> one dies, so dies the other. They all have the same breath *(ruaḥ)*, and
> man has no advantage over the beasts. ... All are (made) from clay, and
> all turn to clay again. Who knows[103] whether the breath *(ruaḥ)* of man
> goes upward and the breath *(ruaḥ)* of the beast goes down to the earth?
>                              (3:19–21, trans. mine)

Sometimes the departure of the life-force and the synonymous
idea of death are combined into a single image or idiom, which
must not be misunderstood to mean that the *nephesh* dies:

> And he (Elijah) asked that he might die (lit. "he asked his *nephesh* to
> die").
>                              (1 Kings 19:4; Jonah 4:8)

> He exposed himself to face death (*NEB;* lit, "he poured out his *nephesh*
> to the death").[104]
>                              (Isa. 53:12)

For the proper understanding of *nephesh mēth* as "corpse" rather
than as "a dead *nephesh*" see above.

c. *The Dead.* The flesh, weakened by the cessation ("departure") of
the life-force, is placed in the tomb, where a minimal continuation

of existence, a mere shadow of the body, was associated with it and especially with the bones. For those who participated in the old cult of the dead, the vitality assigned to the bones of the deceased might be considerable, as in the report of King Ashurbanipal of Assyria concerning his Elamite enemies:

> The graves of their former (and) later kings...I ravaged, destroyed, (and) exposed to the sun. Their bones I took to Assyria. Upon their spirits I imposed restlessness (and) cut them off from food offerings (and) libations of water.[105]

In Israel's normative (canonical) faith, such cultic activity is forbidden and the vitality of the dead reduced almost to the vanishing point. Yet respect for bones and tombs may have continued at least in part as a vestige of that cult. Or perhaps, from a psychological point of view, the bones were preserved because they were the last visible remnant of the deceased, the last physical reminder of their existence.

> Thus says the Lord:
> For three transgressions of Moab, and for four,
> I will not revoke the punishment;
> because he burned to lime the bones of the king of Edom.
>                                                   (Amos 2:1)

> And the bones of Joseph which the people of Israel had brought up from Egypt were buried in Shechem.
>                                                   (Josh. 24:32)

Thus ancient Israel, like their neighbors, strove to keep the bones of family members in a common depository,[106] and used the idiom "to rest with one's fathers" to describe the situation (e.g., 1 Kings 11:43). Whether this idiom reflects a shadowy communal existence in the tomb/underworld, or the physical reality of communal burial, or is merely an equivalent for "N died" is difficult to decide and may have varied from time to time.

It is important to realize that this shadowy remnant of the person (cf. the *eidōlon* of the Homeric Hades and the Akkadian *eṭemmu*) was exactly that: the person reduced to its weakest possible state. It was not a *part* of the person (as if the person were composite) that had escaped the body at death, and it was not identified with the *nephesh* which is said to "go out."[107] It is an image of the body. The usual designation for this (almost non-)entity is *rephaim*, a word whose meaning has been debated but usually is related to the verb "to heal" or "to be weak." Isaiah says of the king of Babylon:

> Sheol beneath is stirred up to meet you when you come,
> it rouses the *shades (rephaim)* to greet you,
>    all who were leaders of the earth;
> . . . . . . . . . . . . . . . . . . . . . . . . . . . .
> All of them will speak and say to you:
> "You too have become as weak as we!
>    You have become like us!"
>
> (14:9–10)

Although a certain amount of vitality and even knowledge is seemingly here attributed to the *rephaim*, it may be only for literary effect, comparable to the use of the word *Sheol*, here personified as a god.[108] The central idea is derision of the king of Babylon: the powerful has become powerless in the extreme. Other biblical texts comment on the status of the *rephaim:*

> Dost thou work wonders for the dead?
> Do the shades rise up to praise thee?
>        (Ps. 88:10 [Hebrew, 11])

> They are dead, they will not live;
>    they are shades, they will not arise;
> to that end thou hast visited them with destruction
>    and wiped out all remembrance of them.
>                    (Isa. 26:14)

## F. REACTION TO INDIVIDUAL BIOLOGICAL DEATH AND TO MORTALITY

Since our primary concern is Israel's psychological and theological reaction to mortality, we must begin by isolating and setting aside certain specific conditions under which impending death seemingly caused inherent anxiety. It is failure to recognize these conditions which has caused some modern scholars to characterize the response to mortality in such terms as these: "The fate of death was greeted by the Israelite not with joy but with fear. The fact that man had to die was seen as oppressive."[109] While it is true that death was not often embraced "with joy," it is far from evident that it was thought to be inherently "oppressive" or unfitting for the human creature.

### 1. A "Bad" Death

Anxiety about biological death seems to have been heightened by any of the following conditions.

a. If it is *premature.* The foreshortening of the human life span, the reduction of its full potential, was regarded as a great evil. Thus David laments when he hears the report concerning his son:

> "Is it well with the young man Absalom?"...And the king was deeply moved (at the negative reply)...and he wept; and...he said, "O my son Absalom, my son, my son Absalom! Would I had died instead of you, O Absalom, my son, my son!"
>
> (2 Sam. 18:32–33)

Similar is King Hezekiah's response when he inquires of the prophet concerning the nature of his illness at age thirty-nine:

> In those days Hezekiah became sick...and Isaiah the prophet...said to him, "Thus says the Lord:...you shall die; you shall not recover." And Hezekiah wept bitterly....(He said:) "In the noontide of my days I must depart;...my dwelling is plucked up and removed from me like a shepherd's tent."
>
> (Isa. 38:1–3, 10, 12)

Similar observations, reactions, and threats are found throughout the literature, such as:

> The godless...die in youth, and their life ends in shame.
>
> (Job 36:13–14)

> I will cut off your strength and the strength of your father's house, so that there will not be an old man in your house.
>
> (1 Sam. 2:31)

Much of the Wisdom Literature (and Prov. 10–31 in particular) gives instruction for the avoidance of premature death:

> The lips of the righteous feed many, but fools die for lack of sense.
>
> (Prov. 10:21)

> He who is steadfast in righteousness will live, but he who pursues evil will die.
>
> (Prov. 11:19)

b. If it is *violent.* Thus Joab, faced with execution, flees to the altar in hope of obtaining sanctuary (1 Kings 2:28–33); Agag the Amalekite, faced with the sword, hopes that the "bitterness of death" has passed (1 Sam. 15:32); Abraham surrenders his wife rather than face the designs of the Pharaoh (Gen. 12:11–13) or the king of Gerar (Gen. 20:2, 10–11); Saul collapses with fear when he learns that he will die in battle the next day (1 Sam. 28:15–20); and various evil persons are threatened with death "by the sword" (e.g., Jeroboam, in Amos 7:11) or with the "death of the slain" (Ezek. 28:8).

Aversion to violent death seems to have been particularly strong if it might involve bloodshed. Such aversion may be a vestige of earlier belief in demons: the life-force (contained in the blood) would drain down into the soil, the realm of the powers of evil.[110] Hence Abel's blood "is crying out from the ground" (Gen. 4:10). The shedding of innocent blood, whether intentional or accidental, came to be regarded as an offense against God and resulted in the "pollution" of the land. Even the shedding of animal blood, except under carefully prescribed conditions, was forbidden,[111] as was the consumption of any blood.[112] Even judicial execution was usually carried out in such fashion as to avoid its loss.[113]

c. If there is *no surviving heir.* Within the context of the older cult of the dead, it was the responsibility of descendants (usually the oldest son)[114] to "call the name" of the ancestors and to provide such offerings at the tomb as were thought necessary for their comfort, lest the "ghosts" be forced to scavenge outside the tomb and be a menace to the living (see chap. 2). ANE adoption contracts sometimes specify that the adoptee shall provide such necessities for their new parent, and this may have been a major motivation for adoption.

In Israel, where the cult of the dead enjoyed no official sanction (at least in the canonical literature)[115] and where it was made most impractical by the concept of an "impurity" resultant from contact with the dead (see above), offspring (and especially sons) were nonetheless appreciated in view of mortality. The firstborn son was given special recognition (e.g., Gen. 27:1–4) and a double portion of the estate.[116] As childless old age approaches, anxiety may be expressed:

> Abram said, "O Lord God, what wilt thou give me, for I continue childless.... Behold, thou hast given me no offspring."
>
> (Gen. 15:2–3)

Conversely, the expectation of offspring is a source of comfort, a divine blessing often compared with long life:

> Your descendants shall be many,
> and your offspring as the grass of the earth.
> You shall come to your grave in ripe old age.
> (Job 5:25–26)

The so-called Suffering Servant is to be consoled by the realization that

> He shall see his offspring,
> he shall prolong his days.
> (Isa. 53:10)

Those who have none to succeed them face the loss of property and, more seriously, of identity:

> Now Absalom in his lifetime had taken and set up for himself the pillar which is in the King's Valley, for he said, "I have no son to keep my name in remembrance"; he called the pillar after his own name, and it is called Absalom's monument to this day.
> (2 Sam. 18:18)

> Let us now sing the praises of famous men,
> . . . . . . . . . . . . . . . . . . . . . . . . . . . . . . . . . . .
> All these won fame in their own generation and were the pride of their
> times.
> . . . . . . . .
> There are others who are unremembered;
> they are dead, and it is as though they had never existed,
> as though they had never been born
> or left children to succeed them.
> (Ecclus. 44:1, 7, 9, *NEB*)

The possibility of such a lamentable fate was combated through a number of institutions, among them adoption,[117] polygamy, concubines through whom a barren wife could satisfy a husband's desire for male offspring,[118] and levirate marriage.[119] In the last-mentioned institution, the widow of a childless man becomes the wife of his brother in order that the resultant children preserve the property and memory of the deceased. This is clearly expressed by Boaz:

> Ruth the Moabitess, the widow of Mahlon, I have bought to be my wife, to perpetuate the name of the dead in his inheritance, that the

name of the dead may not be cut off from among his brethren and from the gate of his native place.

(Ruth 4:10)

## 2. A "Good" Death

The aforementioned protests against certain forms of death are contrasted, even within the Bible itself, with more acceptable forms. Thus the prophet Jeremiah, in comforting King Zedekiah concerning the impending defeat of Jerusalem and the king's resultant capture and exile, tells him that things could be worse:

You shall not die by the sword. You shall die in peace. And as spices were burned for your fathers,...so men shall burn spices for you, and lament for you, saying, "Alas, lord!"

(34:4–5)

And thus the foreigner Balaam says admiringly of Jacob:

Who can count the dust of Jacob,
or number the fourth part of Israel?
Let me die the death of the righteous,
and let my end be like his!
(Num. 23:10)

The ultimate blessing seems to have been to die "in a good old age," as God promised Abraham (Gen. 15:15). Considerable comfort seems to lie behind the oft repeated refrain, "(He) died, an old man and full of years" (e.g., said of Abraham in Gen. 25:8). Similarly Eliphaz, with apparent satisfaction, can describe to Job the good death in store for the righteous, that is, death as God intended it for his creatures:

You shall come to your grave in a ripe old age,
as a shock of grain comes to the threshing floor in its season.
(Job 5:26)

Thus the elderly Jacob, having just learned that his favorite son is yet alive, can now face death without bitterness:

Israel said to Joseph, "I have seen your face again, and you are still alive. Now I am ready to die."

(Gen. 46:30, *NEB*)

Insofar as long life becomes a contributing factor in a "good" death (and it seems to be a central one), then it is mortality itself (the inevitability of death in old age) which becomes acceptable.

### 3. Mortality

Protests against "death" are aimed primarily at those qualities and situations which detract from life lived to the full (illness, alienation, persecution, doubt, and so on) or at a "bad" biological death. They are seldom if ever directed against the appropriateness of death itself.[120] The question "Why should I (or we) die?" is not asked, except in particular circumstances where that immediate fate might be avoided through the proper course of action (e.g., Gen. 47:15). Death at old age does not raise the question of theodicy, in contrast to the misfortunes which may befall one within the bounds of the life span (e.g., in Job's case).[121] The ultimate fate of all humankind is accepted as part of the definition of creaturehood, as part of God's good creation.

> We must all die; we are like water spilt on the ground, which cannot
> be gathered up again.
>
> (2 Sam. 14:14)

There is no suggestion that the meaning of life is thereby called into question, in strong contrast to much modern Western thought.

The creation account in Gen. 1:1—2:4 is so focused upon life, fertility, and goodness (appropriateness?) that the reality of death within that structure is not serious enough even to deserve mention.[122] The human is bracketed with the birds, beasts, and fish on the fifth day of creation, all fashioned of clay and all to clay inevitably and naturally, appropriately, returning.

Even when postexilic prophets looked forward to an ideal age (see below), death was still envisioned as an appropriate part within the divine scheme of things. It did not occur to them (with but rare exception) that death was an evil which should be removed from human experience. However, it would be experienced only after one had enjoyed a full life.

> For behold, I create new heavens and a new earth;
> and the former things shall not be remembered or come to mind.
> But be glad and rejoice for ever in that which I create;
> . . . . . . . . . . . . . . . . . . . . . . . . . . . . . . . . . . . . . . . . . . . . . . . . .

No more shall there be in it an infant that lives but a few days, or an
old man who does not fill out his days,
for the child shall die a hundred years old.

(Isa. 65:17–18, 20)

While premature death is often associated with guilt and punishment, it is not at all clear that such an explanation is made for mortality.[123] Only in the Yahwist's creation account (Genesis 2–3) is
such an explanation possibly to be detected, but even that is debat-
able.[124] It opens the door, however, for such a connection at a later
time in Israel's history (see below, chaps. 5 and 6).

Occasionally, positive aspects of mortality are articulated or alluded to. Thus the couple in the Garden of Eden (Genesis 2–3),
having become rebellious, is forbidden access to "the tree of life."
Death is entirely appropriate for such creatures. Even long life is a
liability:

Then the Lord said, "My breath *(ruaḥ)* shall not abide in man for
ever, for he is flesh, but his days shall be a hundred and twenty years."

(Gen. 6:3, trans. mine)

The realization that death could have a cathartic effect upon society is clear from the explanation for the slowness of Israel's prog-
ress toward the land of Canaan. An entire generation must be
removed from the scene before Israel can realize their destiny.

And the Lord's anger was kindled against Israel, and he made them
wander in the wilderness for forty years, until all the generation that
had done evil in the sight of the Lord was consumed.

(Num. 32:13)

Job, overcome with pain and grief, observes that death would be
a form of release:

Why did I not die at birth,
come forth from the womb and expire?
. . . . . . . . . . . . . . . . . . . . . . . . . . . . . . .
For then I should have lain down and been quiet;
I should have slept; then I would have been at rest...

(3:11–13)

Death is the great equalizer,[125] although it is not clear that Job in his
distress drew much comfort from that reality:

> There (in the underworld) the wicked cease from troubling,
>   and there the weary are at rest.
> There the prisoners are at ease together;
>   they hear not the voice of the taskmaster.
> The small and the great are there,
>   and the slave is free from his master.
>
> (3:17–19)

Anticipation of death can alert humans to the fact that decisions must be made about life; it can serve as an incentive to inquire as to life's ultimate meaning:

> So teach us to number our days that we may get a heart of wisdom.
> (Ps. 90:12)
>
> Enjoy life.... Whatever your hand finds to do, do it with your might!
> (Eccles. 9:9–10)

But that Israel's canonical literature may be described as "mortality-accepting,"[126] or even that positive aspects of that reality can be stressed, is not to deny that negative overtones were sounded. This springs primarily from Israel's covenant understanding—the perception that life has meaning because Yahweh has chosen Israel, delivered them from Egyptian bondage, preserved them in the wilderness, shaped their socioeconomic structure, and willed that they be a "holy people."[127] Thus the psalmist sings of the centrality of God's love, reciting at the sanctuary:

> How precious is thy steadfast love, O God!
> The children of men take refuge in the shadow of thy wings.
> ................................................
> For with thee is the fountain of life;
> and in thy light do we see light.
>
> (36:7, 9)

Thus the pilgrim, anticipating arrival at the temple, could recite:

> As a hart longs for the flowing streams,
> so my soul (*nephesh*, "being") longs for thee, O God.
> (42:1)
>
> How lovely is thy dwelling place, O Lord of hosts!
> My soul (*nephesh*, "being") longs, yea, faints for the courts of the Lord;
> my heart and flesh sing for joy to the living God.
>
> (84:1–2)

Little wonder, then, that death, insofar as it cuts one off from Yahweh's community and concern and renders one weak and forgetful, occasions lament.

> For my soul [*nephesh,* "life"] is full of troubles,
> ....................................
> like one forsaken among the dead,
>   like the slain that lie in the grave,
> like those whom thou dost remember no more.
> ....................................
> Do you work wonders for the dead?
>   Do the shades *(rephaim)* rise up to praise thee?
> Is thy steadfast love declared in the grave?
>   or thy faithfulness in the realm of the dead?
> Are thy wonders known in the darkness,
>   or thy saving help in the land of forgetfulness?
>       (Psalm 88:3-5, 10-12 [Hebrew, 4-6, 11-13])

> For Sheol cannot thank thee,
>   death cannot praise thee;
> those who go down to the pit cannot hope for thy faithfulness.
> The living, the living, he thanks thee, as I do this day.
>       (Isa. 38:18-19)

It should be noted that it is not so much the intrinsic loss of the "I" that is being lamented, not so much mortality as such, as it is the loss of relationship: relationship to a community called to serve God, and relationship with the deity himself.[128] (Some scholars have proposed that such desire for unending relationship with the deity is the foundation for the development of the idea of life after death.)[129]

It is in the Book of Ecclesiastes that mortality comes closest to being a theological problem, although, to be sure, the question of the appropriateness of that universal fate is not raised. Nonetheless, we do have an articulation of the practical problems which death poses, an articulation unique to the canon in its length and intensity.[130]

The author begins by alluding to the individual human life as little more than a momentary image against an enduring backdrop of history:

> A generation goes, and a generation comes, but the earth remains for ever.
>       (1:4)

Given that transitory existence, even the wisest and most accomplished king in Israel's history is forced into an uneasy brooding:

> I made great works... had also great possessions... many concubines, man's delight... surpassed all that were before me in Jerusalem. ...Then I considered all that my hands had done... and behold, all was vanity.
>
> (2:4-11)

Through the exercise of "wisdom" one can avoid premature death, as well as those misfortunes which may metaphorically be characterized as "death"; and yet (biological) death prevails in all cases:

> I saw that wisdom excels folly as light excels darkness... yet I perceived that one fate comes to all of them.
>
> (2:13-14)

But may not one take comfort, as others had proposed, in the memorials which are left behind?

> For of the wise man as of the fool there is no enduring remembrance. ...I hated all my toil... seeing that I must leave it to the man who will come after me; and who knows whether he will be a wise man or a fool?
>
> (2:16-19)

And thus if comfort is to be found, it must be found in the present moment as opposed to taking satisfaction in that which one leaves behind:

> There is nothing better for a man than that he should eat and drink, and find enjoyment in his toil.
>
> (2:24a)

Such enjoyment, while temporary, is itself a positive value. Moreover, it need not be seen as mere sensate enjoyment, but as existence which the Creator-God has provided:

> This also, I saw, was from the hand of God; for apart from him, who can eat or who can have enjoyment?
>
> (2:24b)

Everything therefore has a "season," death as well as birth (3:1-2), each of them appropriate to the Creator's design (3:11). True wisdom therefore is to be found in the acceptance of that which God has given: life, with its possibilities and its limitations (3:12–14). And thus does the author overcome nihilism by keeping death within the domain of God's wisdom. Human creatureliness is manifest both in limitations and in acceptance of the deity's design "that men should fear before him" (3:14).

### 4. Coping with Death

How were the ancient Israelites (Yahwists) able to cope with mortality, apparently successfully? In addition to the aforementioned factors which contributed to a "good" death (old age, offspring), at least the following realities were supportive.

1. The God who has chosen Israel and made promises to them was regarded by his people as the sole effective divine power. There was thus no need to fear capricious deities or demons with an intrinsic power of their own. It is the one God, benign toward his people, and he alone, who has set the bounds of human life. The life-force is not only his power at work, but it is he who commands it to "return." Hence individuals could pray to die, even prematurely, secure in their faith that Yahweh was Lord of life and death:

> And he (Elijah) asked that he might die, saying, "It is enough; now, O Lord, take away my life."
>
> (1 Kings 19:4)

> And the sons of the prophets...came out to Elisha, and said to him, "Do you not know that today the Lord will take away your master from over you?"
>
> (2 Kings 2:3; cf. 5, 9)

Having been informed of the sudden death of his children, Job remarks,

> The Lord gave, and the Lord has taken away; blessed be the name of the Lord.[131]
>
> (1:21)

Death therefore was not an irrational, intruding enemy but part of an ordered, controlled, harmonious creation. Biological life and death are not separate phenomena, as if the latter intruded to thwart the Creator's design. They are bound together as part of a singular divine will for his creatures. To accept one is to accept the other; to despise one is to despise the other. Mortality likely would not have been part of the script which humans would have written for themselves; they may lament separation from Yahweh's worshiping community, but for those able to acknowledge Yahweh's sovereignty, it seems to have been acceptable.

2. Israel's political history and the geography of the area combined to produce a mentality in which the welfare of the group predominated over that of the individual.[132] That the individual perished was not an ultimate loss, since the group would survive. Moreover, Israel's survival was not a mere human value: it was understood to be the will of God. Not only had the Deity called and preserved the group: their destiny had not yet been fully realized. God had promised[133] his people a land, a flourishing population, and that they would be a blessing[134] (Gen. 12:1-3), a "realm of priests and a holy nation" (Exod. 19:6). Thus Abraham's anxiety about the absence of offspring, at least as the larger context presents it, is not that he will be forgotten but that the promise will not be realized: God's Israel will not come into being. In any case he seems content to realize that aspects of the promise will not come to pass in his lifetime: "To your descendants I will give this land" (Gen. 12:7; cf. 13:14-16). And as one of his last acts he secures a wife for his son so that the promise will continue to be recited and made manifest (24:1-9).

The aged Jacob, nearly blind, announces to the comfort of his heirs and to his own satisfaction,

> Behold, I am about to die, but God will be with you, and will bring you again to the land of your fathers.
>
> (Gen. 48:21)

Similarly, when the great man Moses is about to die, no resentment toward that reality is evident—only remorse that he will not live to enter the land with the people Israel (Deut. 34:1-8; 3:23-28; Num. 20:1-13).[135] His concluding admonitions to the people stress the continuity of God's promise and thus of Israel's life:

> The Lord has said to me, "You shall not go over this Jordan." The Lord your God himself will go over before you.
>
> (Deut. 31:2-3)

3. It is faith in the ongoing life of God's people which provides a context for the realization of other values, values which make it possible to accept mortality with greater ease. Not only does the community enhance the security of one's offspring who are to remember their deceased ancestors lest their "name" perish (Ps. 41:5; see above), but it also provides a setting wherein one's reputation may be preserved, whether by offspring or not.

> The memory of the righteous is a blessing,
> but the name of the wicked will rot.
> (Prov. 10:7)

It must be noted that the desire for offspring and reputation need not always be motivated by self-interest; it is not always the preservation of the "I" that is desired or which gives the greatest comfort. Thus Ben Sirach sings the praises of "famous men" who have been the instrument of God and have built up the community:

> Let us now sing the praises of famous men,
> the heroes of our nation's history,
> *through whom the Lord established his renown,*
> and revealed his majesty in each succeeding age.
> . . . . . . . . . . . . . . . . . . . . . . . . . . . . . . . . . . . . .
> Thanks to them *their children are within the covenants—*
> the whole race of their descendants.
> Their line will endure for all time,
> and their fame will never be blotted out.
> (Ecclus. 44:1–2, 12–13, *NEB,* emphasis mine)

Even the persons without offspring could participate in the ongoing life of the community, through their influence, and be comforted:

> And the eunuch must not say,
> "I am nothing but a barren tree."
> For these are the words of the Lord:
> "The eunuchs who keep my sabbaths,
> and who choose to do my will and hold fast to my covenant,
> shall receive from me something better than sons and daughters:
> a memorial and a name in my house and within my walls.
> I will give them an everlasting name,
> a name imperishable for all time."[136]
> (Isa. 56:3–5, *NEB*)

4. When separation from the covenant community and its Deity by means of death (metaphoric or biological) is anticipated, one's complaint may take a specific form in communal recitation. Concerning the OT's prayers of lament, it has been observed that "such regularized speech activity serves both to *enhance* the experience so that dimensions of it are not lost and to *limit* the experience so that some dimensions are denied their legitimacy ... so that it can be received and coped with according to the perspectives, perceptions, and resources of the community. Thus the function of the form is definitional. It tells the experiencer the shape of the experience which it is legitimate to experience."[137] Within a community which has a history of interaction with the Deity, the worshiper is moved from an isolated sense of negativity and chaos to a communal assertion of affirmation. In case of "metaphoric" or premature biological death, the affirmation takes the form of the expectation or proclamation[138] of deliverance (return to "life"); in the case of mortality (which is much rarer), what is affirmed is that God is present, sovereign, righteous, and worthy of praise.[139]

It is in Psalm 90 that human transience and divine permanence are set in the starkest contrast. Through its recitation, the community is enabled to state the former reality without engendering resentment, accusation of injustice on God's part, or even pessimism. Rather, one finds a description of the human situation interspersed with praises of God's eternal being, as if mortality is noteworthy in that it enhances one's awe and appreciation of that which does endure. And thus the psalm moves toward its conclusion:

> So teach us to number our days that we may get a heart of wisdom.
> .............................................................
> Satisfy us in the morning with thy steadfast love,
> that we may rejoice and be glad all our days.
>
> (vv. 12, 14)

Concerning this majestic psalm, so profound and powerful that tradition uniquely attributed it among the psalms to Moses, Weiser has correctly observed:

> the awareness of man's mortality does not arise ... from the despon-

dent frame of mind of a man whose pessimistic outlook is entirely rooted in this world, but is oriented on the thought of God's eternal being. . . . in view of the transitoriness of life he seeks and finds permanent support in God. . . . his concern is to experience God himself; and that experience to him means joy in life.[140]

# CHAPTER 4

# The Transition toward

# Apocalyptic Eschatology

### *The Context for a New Evaluation*
### *of Mortality*

Beginning during the early postexilic period (sixth to fifth century B.C.) there was in some quarters a shift of thought toward apocalyptic eschatology[1] from the prophetic eschatology which had characterized much of the previous literature. It was a shift which would ultimately result in a new evaluation of the appropriateness of mortality within the theological scheme of things.

By *prophetic eschatology* one may denote the conviction that present Israelite society must be reformed. The reformation will take place within the arena of history, hopefully in response to the exhortation of the prophets themselves, but if necessary as the result of divine discipline through the immediate instrumentality of the forces of nature or international politics (invasion, defeat, exile). Such unsettling events would, if perceived in the appropriate theological context, bring Israel into conformity with their ancient ideals.

By *apocalyptic eschatology* (a separable spectrum within the wider and historically later theological perspective called apocalypticism) one may denote the conviction that current human abilities, political structures, and historical forces are insufficient to affect the transformation which Yahweh desires. There is a loss of confidence in human institutions and in human ability to reform them. Only direct action by the Deity will be sufficient.[2]

From the earliest period downward, Israel's canonical literature attests the difficulty of maintaining their collective identity in view of the tensions between their theology, with its unique socioeconomic values, and that of the surrounding cultures.[3] Hindrances seem to have been of two primary sorts:

a. Internal: human nature, with its tendencies to forget the blessings and the dangers of the past:

> You shall remember what the Lord your God did to Pharaoh and to all Egypt...
>
> (Deut. 7:18)

> Remember... how you provoked the Lord your God to wrath in the wilderness.... And now, Israel, what does the Lord your God require of you, but to fear the Lord your God...?
>
> (Deut. 9:7; 10:12)

Such failure of memory and gratitude was often coupled with a tendency toward rebellion and the desire to follow one's own inclinations.

> For I know how rebellious and stubborn you are.
>
> (Deut. 31:27)

> This evil people, who refuse to hear my words, who stubbornly follow their own heart and have gone after other gods to serve them and worship them...
>
> (Jer. 13:10)

This aspect of Israel's identity problem was addressed through such means as negative (e.g., Exod. 22:18—23:13) and positive (e.g., Exod. 21:1—22:17) guidelines for behavior, undergirded by divine sanction (e.g., Exod. 21:23-24); amulets or other physical identity-reminders (e.g., tassels on garments, Num. 15:37-41); the radical excision of individuals or groups who posed a threat to the community (e.g., Deut. 13:5, where a death penalty is to be enacted so that "you shall purge the evil from the midst of you"); the recitation of stories which depicted both the faithfulness (Genesis 22) and the unfaithfulness (Genesis 12 and 17) of the ancestors;[4] and a separate group ("tribe") whose function it was to teach "the way of the Lord" (the Levites "shall teach Jacob thy ordinances, and Israel thy law," Deut. 33:10).

b. External: historical reverses which challenged the group's self-understanding. Israel's early sacred literature focuses upon the patron Deity of the group, a Deity who was believed to have entered into a covenant which involved the promise of offspring, land, and "blessing."[5] Rather than focusing upon the interaction of divine forces whose function it was to regulate the processes of nature (as in the Canaanite Baal Epic) or upon cosmic legitimization of contemporary royal power structures (as in the Sumerian Kinglist), Israel began with the claim that their ancestor had been called and commissioned, thereby founding an enduring community which would be distinct from their neighbors. They would be "a kingdom of priests and a holy nation" (Exod. 19:6) to whom all the nations would come in order to learn the way of the Lord (Isa. 2:1–4; Mic. 4:1–3).[6] Events of history often seemed to support that self-understanding and indeed may have helped to generate it: safe migration of the ancestor to Canaan[7] (Gen. 12), deliverance from Egyptian bondage; survival in the wilderness (Numbers); conquest of the land (Joshua), and the military and economic successes of the early monarchy. Thus a chain of events could be constructed, leading from promise to fulfillment (Abraham in the land, with offspring), to re-fulfillment (return to the land under Joshua), and to fulfillment once again (the return from Exile: see esp. Isa. 51:2–3).

Events which seemed to challenge this self-understanding could nonetheless be incorporated into the framework: the barrenness of the patriarchal wives illustrates God's ability to keep his promises, even when it seemed most unlikely (Genesis 17); famine drives Jacob and his descendants out of the "promised land," but God nonetheless makes long-range provision for his people (Gen. 45:5–8); slavery in Egypt sets the stage for a miraculous deliverance, central to most subsequent theology; inability to enter the "promised land" at the time of Moses and Joshua, in part because of enemy resistance, provides opportunity for a new, more worthy generation to mature to the task (Num. 32:13); long-lasting pockets of resistance to Israel's presence in the "promised land" are a divinely ordained means of discipline (Judg. 2:20—3:2); the division of the Davidic kingdom, an ultimately fatal state of affairs in view of Assyrian and Babylonian expansionist policies, could be justified as punishment for the excesses of the rule of Solomon (1 Kings 11:26–40).

It is in the thought of the prophets that one finds a sustained grappling with the problems for Israel's identity posed by the aforementioned internal and external threats.

a. On the one hand, they will plead with the people to change their priorities, to abide by the ancient ideals:

> Seek good, and not evil,
>     that you may live;
> and so the Lord, the God of hosts, will be with you,
>     as you have said.
> Hate evil, and love good,
>     and establish justice in the gate.
>
> (Amos 5:14–15)

> Turn now, every one of you, from his evil way and wrong doings, and dwell upon the land which the Lord has given to you and to your fathers from of old and for ever.
>
> (Jer. 25:5)

Some of the prophets seem to have regarded such exhortation as futile and repentance as temporary:

> Were I to write for him (Israel) my laws by ten thousands, they would (still) be regarded as a strange thing.
>
> (Hos. 8:12)

> (Israel says,) "Come, let us return to the Lord...." (Yahweh responds,) "What shall I do with you, O Ephraim?... Your love is like a morning cloud, like the dew that goes early away."
>
> (Hos. 6:1, 4)

Others hoped for a time of spontaneous obedience:

> Behold, the days are coming, says the Lord, when... I will put my law within them, and I will write it upon their hearts; and I will be their God, and they shall be my people. And no longer shall each man teach his neighbor and each his brother saying, "Know the Lord," for they shall all know me, from the least of them to the greatest.
>
> (Jer. 31:31, 33–34)

b. On the other hand, they proposed that historical reverses were part of God's "discipline"[8] in order to transform his people:

> I gave you cleanness of teeth in all your cities... I also withheld the rain from you... I smote you with blight and mildew... I sent among you a pestilence... I overthrew some of you... yet you did not return to me.
>
> (Amos 4:6, 7, 9, 10, 11)

In view of the failure of such limited attempts at eliciting the desired response, the prophets proposed that it would now be necessary for Yahweh to dismantle all existing institutions, to take away the land, and to reinstitute conditions similar to Egyptian bondage:

> They shall not remain in the land of the Lord;
>> but Ephraim shall return to Egypt,
>> and they shall eat unclean food in Assyria.
>> (Hos. 9:3)

> Therefore, behold, I will allure her,
>> and bring her into the wilderness,
>> and speak tenderly to her.
> . . . . . . . . . . . . . . . . . . . . . . .
> And there she shall answer as in the days of her youth,
>> as at the time when she came out of the land of Egypt.
>> (Hos. 2:14–15 [Hebrew, 16–17])

> I will turn my hand against you, and will melt away your dross as with lye and remove all your alloy. And I will restore your judges as at the first, and your counselors as at the beginning.
> (Isa. 1:25–26)

The prophets, then, were convinced that Yahweh's actions and intentions could be perceived within the arena of history, in events negative as well as positive: "History is the goal-directed conversation of the Lord of the future with Israel."[9]

However, the severity of the destruction wrought by the conquering Assyrians (721, 701 B.C.) and Babylonians (597, 587 B.C.), as well as the inevitably attendant diseases, must have been a shock even to those able to acknowledge the sovereignty of God in the events (Lamentations). And thus a disciple of Isaiah, active during the Babylonian exile (587–539 B.C.), probably expressed a common sentiment when he remarked that Israel had "received from the Lord's hand double for all her sins" (Isa. 40:2). For those whose theological foundations included the claim that God had made an everlasting covenant with David and his descendants (2 Samuel 7), with the corollary idea of the inviolability of Mt. Zion where temple and palace were located (Psalm 132), the shock of exile would have been especially severe, bordering on renunciation of Yahwism as a viable faith. It was only with difficulty, therefore, that this "Second Isaiah" (chaps. 40–55) could arouse a sense of identity and trust sufficient to prepare for a return to the "promised land."

Although recent events seemed to some observers within the community to have demonstrated Yahweh's impotence, the prophet insisted that God had been and was still active in world events, citing such possibilities as the conquests of Cyrus the Persian (Isa. 41:2–4). That is merely the first step, however, in the bold divine plan which the prophet unveils to his doubting audience:

> Speak tenderly to Jerusalem,
>   and cry to her that her warfare is ended . . .
> . . . . . . . . . . . . . . . . . . . . . . . . . . . . . . . . . . . . . . . .
> A (heavenly) voice cries:
> "In the wilderness prepare the way of the Lord,
>   make straight in the desert a highway for our God."
>                                         (40:2–3)

> And he said to me, "You are my servant,
>   Israel, in whom I will be glorified. . . .
> I will give you as a light to the nations,
>   that my salvation may reach to the ends of the earth."
>                                         (49:3, 6)

In order to enhance the believability of his vision, the prophet seeks to widen his audience's perception of the range of Yahweh's activity, both as Creator of the world and in the great events of Israel's past. One of the ways that he does this is to allude to ancient stories of Yahweh's conflict with and victory over opponents, both semidivine and human.[10] For example, while not preserved in sustained form in the canonical literature, there are allusions in the temple liturgy to his victory over the forces of chaos at creation:

> Thou didst crust the heads of Leviathan,[11]
>   thou didst give him as food for the creatures of the wilderness.
>                                         (Ps. 74:14)

> Thou didst crush Rahab like a carcass,
>   thou didst scatter thy enemies with thy mighty arm.
>                                         (Ps. 89:10 [Hebrew, 11])

Or again, there were ancient accounts of Yahweh's earth-shattering theophany, in the form of a divine warrior,[12] to fight for his people:

> Lord, when thou didst go forth from Seir,
> when thou didst march from the region of Edom,
> the earth trembled . . . the mountains quaked . . .
> . . . . . . . . . . . . . . . . . . . . . . . . . . . . . . . . . . . . . . . .

The kings came, they fought;
then fought the kings of Canaan,
..............................
From heaven fought the stars,
from their courses they fought against Sisera.
                              (Judg. 5:4–5, 19–20)

The Lord came from Sinai,
  and dawned from Seir upon us;
he shone forth from Mount Paran,
he came from the ten thousands of holy ones,
  with flaming fire at his right hand.
                              (Deut. 33:2)

Such traditions now became a paradigm for understanding the present:

Awake, awake, put on strength, O arm of the Lord;
awake, as in days of old, the generations of long ago.
Was it not thou that didst cut Rahab in pieces,
  that didst pierce the dragon?
Was it not thou that didst dry up the sea,
  the waters of the great deep;
that didst make the depths of the sea a way for the redeemed to pass
  over?
And the ransomed of the Lord shall return,
  and come with singing to Zion.
                              (Isa. 51:9–11)

In his application of such materials to the contemporary situation, the prophet is both traditional and innovative: *(a)* traditional in that God's activity is still to be discerned within the ordinary-appearing events of international politics (history), some recent events with short-range implications to the contrary; *(b)* innovative in that ancient conflict-myths, deemphasized by prior prophets, are used as guidelines for understanding the present.

That portion of the community in exile which found the prophet's interpretation of history and vision for the future believable[13] returned home, many of them to find that the vision did not accord with reality. They encountered economic hardship, hostility from their Judean kinsmen who had not been forced into exile, internal strife, harassment from neighboring areas, and military domination by the Persians, of whose empire their homeland was but a province. Many accepted the realities of life as a vassal state and turned to a theocratic model of government based upon a completed pentateuch as "constitution," under the leadership of Aaronide priests.[14] It was a divinely ordained, perpetual form of government, God's rule among his people—internal problems and foreign domination notwithstanding. Thus Ben Sirach centuries later could sing lyrically of the joys which the Aaronide system aroused (Ecclus. 50:1–21; cf. 45:6–22). Others within the community, however, apparently "outsiders" to the structures of power and perhaps oppressed by them,[15] increasingly lost faith in history as the arena where God's activity could be detected or anticipated. Hindrance to the proper (divine) order was extended from groups within the community (Isaiah 58; 59) and neighboring states (Isaiah 63) to the entire world:

> Behold, the Lord will lay waste the earth and make it desolate, he will twist its surface and scatter its inhabitants.... The earth lies polluted under its inhabitants, for they have transgressed the laws, violated the statutes, broken the everlasting covenant.
>
> (Isa. 24:1, 5)

Hope therefore could not lie in a this-worldly transformation of "real" politics, but rather must come from the outside. Rather than being delivered *through* (or *within*) history, one must now be delivered *from* it. Such hope was to be found in the same images of the ancient conflict-myths which the "Second Isaiah" had utilized. But his disciples (collectively called the Third Isaiah), whose thoughts are found predominately in Isaiah chaps. 56–66, rather than seeing in such material suggestive images for the interpretation of history literalized them into a solution of the problem of history: victory would come directly at the hands of the divine warrior.

> O that thou wouldst rend the heavens and come down,
> that the mountains might quake at thy presence!
> . . . . . . . . . . . . . . . . . . . . . . . . . . . . . . . . . . . . . . . . . . . . .
> to make thy name known to thy adversaries,
> and that the nations might tremble at thy presence!
> . . . . . . . . . . . . . . . . . . . . . . . . . . . . . . . . . . . . . . . . . . . . .
> From of old no one has heard or perceived by ear,
> no eye has seen a God beside thee, who works for those who wait for
>   him.
>
> (Isa. 64:1–4)

It was often anticipated that following his victory Yahweh would give a banquet for the faithful (again, an ancient motif). Sometimes the benefits are restricted so that often they are to be extended only to the visionary's group. Any subsequent influence upon the nations, if not sense of vocation to them such as was found in the Second Isaiah, thus decreases as a concern.[16]

In some conceptions the present oppressed righteous will physically enter into the conflict, will participate with the heavenly warrior in routing the foe. Thus Zech. 10:5,

> They shall fight because the Lord is with them,
> and they shall confound the riders on horses.

How is death envisioned and responded to in this type of OT literature? Very much as it is in the materials already studied:

1. The term continues to be used as a metaphor for those things which hinder full life, and especially on a collective level. Thus it is used to describe the exilic and postexilic community: defeated and harassed from without, divided and demoralized within. Ezekiel's vision of restoration makes such metaphor clear:

> "Son of man, can these bones live?... Behold, I will cause breath to enter you, and you shall live." ... Then he said to me, "Son of man, these bones are the whole house of Israel.... Behold, I will open your graves, and raise you from your graves, O my people; and I will bring you home to the land of Israel."
>
> (37:3, 5, 11, 12)

Less clear, on the surface, is the Second Isaiah's use of such language to describe the community:

> Behold, my servant shall prosper,
> ............................
> By oppression and judgment he was taken away;
> ... who considered that he was cut off out of the land of the living...?
> And they made his grave with the wicked,
> ...................................
> Therefore I will divide him a portion with the great...
> because he poured out his soul (*nephesh*, "life") to death...
>
> (Isa. 52:13; 53:8-9, 12)

Less unanimity of interpretation can be found for a slightly later passage, describing oppressed elements of the community in similar terms:

> Let your dead ones live![17]
> Let your[18] corpses rise!
> Let those who dwell in the dust arouse[19] and rejoice!
> Thy dew is the dew of the Fields;[20]
> Let it fall on the land of the Shades *(rephaim)*!
> Go, my people! Enter your dwellings!
> Lock the doors behind you;
> Hide for a little while, until the wrath is past!
>                          (Isa. 26:19–20, trans. William Millar)

2. When applied to biological cessation and to mortality, there continues to be no negative reaction (save in the two relatively late cases noted below, and as qualified below). And thus when the Third Isaiah envisions the renewal of creation and thereby conditions under which full "life" in the community will be possible, mortality remains the proper condition of human existence. That limitation is simply not a part of Israel's (or the world's) current problem! Even if Israel's anthropology would allow it, which would be difficult enough (see above), there continues to be no generally perceived theological problem sufficient to cause a move toward the eradication of mortality.

> For behold, I create new heavens and a new earth;
> and the former things shall not be remembered or come to mind.
> . . . . . . . . . . . . . . . . . . . . . . . . . . . . . . . . . . . . . . . . . . . . . . . . . . . . . . . . . .
> No more shall there be in it an infant that lives but a few days,
> or an old man who does not fill out his days;
> for the child shall die a hundred years old,
> and the one who does not attain this (minimum) will be regarded as
>     accursed.
>                          (65:17, 20; RSV except 20b$\beta$)

3. In one relatively late text,[21] "death" seems to be regarded as a power which will be defeated as part of the divine warrior's victory. (Or is it merely a common noun: a condition which must be removed because it would mar the joy of that victory?) Just as the Canaanite god Baal had thrown a victory banquet after his defeat of Yamm (Sea), and just as he had struggled with the god Mot (Death) and ultimately asserted his sovereignty, so perhaps Yahweh is envisioned as reestablishing his power over the forces of chaos.

The underworld (Sheol), sometimes having been described as "swallowing" *(bāla‘)* persons at death (Num. 16:32; 26:10; Ps. 69:15; Prov. 1:12), will itself now be consumed *(bāla‘).*

> Yahweh of Hosts has made
> For all peoples on this mount:
> A feast of oil;
> A feast of wine;
> Fat, well cured;
> The best of wine.
> He will swallow on this mount
> The net ensnared
> About all the people;
> The web woven
> About all the nations.
> He will swallow death forever.
> He will wipe the tears
> From all faces.
> The reproach of his people he will remove
> From all the earth.[22]
>
> (Isa. 25:6–8)

Whether the crucial line ("He will swallow death forever") is original to the poem has been debated, and usually denied.[23] In any case, it is unclear whether it was a literal expectation or poetic exaggeration (comparable to "the lion shall eat straw like the ox," Isa. 11:7). Another way of putting it might be, are we dealing with *affirmation* or with *aspiration?* Moreover, the vision concerns those then living; it does not concern itself with the fate of those already dead, that is, with resurrection.

It is only in the Book of Daniel, generally acknowledged to have taken shape early in the second century B.C., that the doctrine of a resurrection of the dead makes its appearance. We read of battles in heaven between the angelic "princes" of Persia (10:13) and Greece (10:20) on the one hand and the angelic "prince" of the Jews named Michael (10:21) on the other[24]—battles which are heavenly prototypes of struggles on earth, and in which the earthly "people of the saints (lit. "holy ones") of the Most High" (7:27; cf. 8:24) join forces with the heavenly "saints (lit "holy ones") of the Most High" (7:21–22).[25] As the struggle nears its completion we read,

Many of those who sleep in the dust of the earth shall awake, some to everlasting life, and some to shame and everlasting contempt. And those who are wise shall shine like the brightness of the firmament; and those who turn many to righteousness, like the stars for ever and ever.

(12:2-3)

The precise reason for this resurrection is not stated. However, since only Jews are involved, and even then only those at the extremes of wickedness and righteousness ("many...some"), it seems to be tied up with internal strife rather than mortality as a general theological problem. We are not explicitly told that death will thereafter be removed as an inevitable human experience. Furthermore, it is important to notice that the angelic forces in opposition to Michael are not identified as intrinsically evil, and least of all are they identified with a "devil" who is responsible for human evil and death. But that identification will be made in the Intertestamental literature and in the New Testament.

One other antecedent of subsequent thought may also be noticed. Since the earthly "saints" have joined force with the heavenly "saints," and since, in one scholarly interpretation at least, the resurrected righteous are elevated to heaven for permanent union with the angels ("(they)...shall shine...like the stars"),[26] it is understandable that later persecuted groups, like those at Qumran, would describe themselves as *already* members of the heavenly assembly.

# CHAPTER 5

# The Intertestamental

# Literature

## A. FACTORS THAT CONTRIBUTE TO A
## NEW VIEW OF LIFE AFTER DEATH

By the second century B.C., apocalyptic eschatology has in some quarters become the core of a much wider religious perspective known as apocalypticism,[1] a perspective which increasingly includes hope for transcendence of death, but not as an end in itself (see below, no. 4). A number of factors may have combined to foster such hope.

1. Israel's ancient conflict-myths, reused to interpret the difficulties of the present (see chap. 4). Yahweh's opponents could now be perceived to include the demons which characterized the faith of Israel's neighbors and indeed had played a role in Israel's own pre-Yahwistic faith and their continuing folk religion. Having previously been denied autonomy, potency, or even existence, they could now be reactivated within an orthodox framework of Yahweh's sovereignty. And thus the misfortunes of the world, including death, could be explained, and their defeat anticipated.

> God created man to rule the world, and appointed for him two spirits ...all who practice perversity are under the domination of the Angel of Darkness and walk in ways of Darkness.... even those who practice righteousness are made liable to error. All their sins and their iniquities, all their guilt and their deeds of transgression are the result of his domination; and this, by God's inscrutable design, will continue until the time appointed by Him. Moreover, all men's afflictions and all their moments of tribulation are due to this being's malevolent sway.
>
> (1 QS III, 17–22)[2]

2. The influence of foreign eschatologies, and that of the Persians

in particular. Such influence would seem likely, given the fact that they exercised political domination over Judah for approximately two hundred years. Their religion was characterized by a thorough-going cosmic and ethical dualism, including a resurrection and judgment of the dead.[3] It seems likely, however, that such outside influence, rather than inciting Israel to otherwise unlikely specula-tions, largely served to clarify and expand the application of their own ancient mythology.[4]

3. The repeated affirmation in Israel's literature from the earliest time downward, in covenant formulations and in Wisdom Liter-ature, that Yahweh wills "life" and not "death" for his people. Such metaphoric usage of the terms could now be applied especially to biological categories: all forms of "death" could be regarded as evil.[5]

> Do not stray from the path of life and so court death.... For God did not make death, and takes no pleasure in the destruction of any living thing.[6]
> (Wisd. of Sol. 1:12–13, *NEB*)

> But God created man for immortality, and made him in the image of his own eternal self; it was the devil's spite that brought death into the world, and the experience of it is reserved for those who take his side.
> (Wisd. of Sol. 2:23–24, *NEB*)

At the end of the former quotation one may hear an echo of Ezek. 18:32, "For I have no pleasure in the death of anyone, says the Lord God; so turn, and live." The prophet speaks of premature death, but the author of the Wisdom of Solomon has expanded it to include other categories, including mortality.

4. "Life," as the OT sees it, involves relatedness in community. Thus if such communal life, including the actualization of its values, be-comes increasingly difficult because of Seleucidian oppression,[7] then drastic action on God's part may be necessary in order to free the community for the realization of its potential. It is within this con-text that a biblical doctrine of life after death must be understood. It is not an isolated event, a mere "grave-emptying" operation,[8] but part of a complex of end-time events.[9] It is important to realize that modern popular expectations, when they are visualized as an end in themselves (as the mere preservation of the "self" in heaven), have largely forsaken their biblical antecedents. (For continuing emphasis upon the larger complex see below, p. 90.)

5. The idea that human sinfulness causes premature death, found especially in Israel's Wisdom Literature, could lead to the conclusion that death itself (mortality) was a consequence of a sinful human condition. If that human condition could be overcome, then death would be deprived of its reason for existence. Such grappling with the need to improve the human disposition is evident in prophetic language about a time of spontaneous obedience (Jer. 31:31–34) and in the anticipation of a "new heart" (Ezek. 18:31; 36:26). The creation account in Genesis 2–3, with its etiology (or etiologies—see chap. 3) concerning death, could be read in such fashion as to support the perspective that it is a manifestation of a "fall" which has affected all subsequent generations.

> Woman is the origin of sin, and it is through her that we all die.
> (Ecclus. 25:24, *NEB*)

This perspective, with a shift in gender, will be repeated in later literature:

> As in Adam all men die, so in Christ all will be brought to life.
> (1 Cor. 15:22, *NEB*)

> For the first man, Adam, was burdened with a wicked heart; he sinned and was overcome, and not only he but all his descendants.
> (2 Esd. 3:21, *NEB*)

6. A more "developed" anthropology, perhaps under the influence of the Greeks under whose political influence the Judeans came in the late fourth century B.C. In some of the "mystery religions" of the sixth century B.C. and afterward, the life principle *(psuchē)*[10] was fused with the principle of consciousness and memory *(thumos),* resulting in an entity[11] which was thought capable of surviving cessation of bodily functions. Again, such outside influence may only have enhanced forces already at work in Israelite thought. Once biological death is identified with the forces of chaos which Yahweh will defeat (Isa. 25:8), then the question of the status of those already dead will arise: Will they participate in the joys and judgments of the postvictory age? This is solved in a variety of fashions, generally involving resurrection (Daniel 12). And that subsequently raises the question of their status in the interim between death and resurrection: Are they largely unaware of their surroundings, only semiexistent, as in the traditional picture of

Sheol? Or fully conscious and affected by events on earth, as in the pre-Yahwistic cult of the dead? In the Intertestamental literature an increasing measure of awareness is assigned to them in an intermediate abode. In some cases, however, the righteous apparently are transported immediately at death to the realm of the gods with memory fully intact.[12]

## B. REACTIONS TO AND EVALUATIONS OF BIOLOGICAL DEATH

In the literature of the OT instances of biological death, whether premature, violent, or peacefully occurring in old age, are reported laconically. Now the descriptions become sustained and graphic, indicating not merely the realities and uncertainties of life under the oppressive Seleucids but also that death itself is being perceived as a problem.

1. Death may be a blessing, since it releases one from further suffering. The persecution of the "righteous" at the hands of Antiochus Epiphanes was sustained and of unusual severity. Hence the author of Daniel speaks of persons being thrown alive into a "burning fiery furnace" (3:11) or into a den of lions (chap. 6); of a beast with iron teeth which "devoured and broke in pieces" (7:7). Premature and violent death, previously often regarded as a sign of sinfulness and divine displeasure, now seemed to be the norm for those who remained faithful to Yahwism in the face of pressure to conform to Hellenistic culture. Experience now seemed to indicate that suffering was in direct proportion to one's adherence to the faith and practice of the fathers. And thus the Wisdom of Solomon (first century) reverses traditional theology concerning sin and suffering: the premature death of the righteous indicates that they were worthy of the divine presence (3:4–5) and frees them from further suffering.

> But the good man, even if he dies an untimely death, will be at rest. For it is not length of life and number of years which bring the honour due to age; if men have understanding, they have grey hairs enough, and an unspotted life is the true ripeness of age. There was once such a man who pleased God. ... He was snatched away before his mind could be perverted by wickedness or his soul deceived by falsehood. ... His soul was pleasing to the Lord, who removed him early from a wicked world.
>
> (4:7–14, *NEB*)

In a strange variation on this perspective, the Testament of Abraham alludes to the advantage of premature death even for the wicked. Whereas in the canonical literature such death was regarded as a great misfortune (punishment for sin which might have been avoided, since Yahweh wills life rather than death), it now assumes a positive aspect in view of the expectation of judgment after death. Premature death is sufficient compensation for sinfulness and thus might relieve one's anxiety concerning further punishment. Speaking of Abraham's servants who died prematurely (as the result of looking upon the undisguised face of "Death") God says:

> I have called (them) back to life... because for a time I have requited them in judgment. But I do not requite in death those whom I destroy living upon the earth.
>
> (chap. 14, end)

2. Death may be an occasion for witnessing to the faith, especially in the case of martyrdom.[13] By willing acceptance of death rather than conforming to the will of apostates, one can have a "good" death. In earlier canonical literature, on the other hand, a "good" death usually referred to a quite different manner of death—for example, nonviolent and at an advanced age. Now it frequently presupposed violence. And thus the pious Eleazar, aged ninety, refuses to escape death through a pretended consumption of forbidden food:

> Send me quickly to my grave. If I went through with this pretense at my time of life, many of the young might believe that at the age of ninety Eleazar had turned apostate. If I practiced deceit..., I should lead them astray and bring stain and pollution on my old age.... So if I now die bravely, I shall... leave the young a fine example, to teach them how to die a good death, gladly and nobly, for our revered and holy laws.
>
> (2 Macc. 6:23–28, *NEB*)

3. Hope of resurrection is explicitly cited as awaiting the righteous who resist apostasy. It is sufficient compensation for the martyrdom now endured. And thus the third of seven martyred sons, when asked if he would renounce the faith,

> boldly held out his hands, and said courageously: "The God of heaven gave me these. His laws mean far more to me than they do, and it is from him that I trust to receive them back."

Their mother had encouraged them thusly:

> It is the Creator of the universe who moulds man at his birth and plans the origin of all things. Therefore he, in his mercy, will give you back life and breath again, since now you put his laws above all thought of self.
>
> (2 Macc. 7:10–11, 23, *NEB*)

4. Death is an ultimate threat only to the wicked, who assume that death is the end of meaningful existence.

> They said to themselves in their deluded way: "Our life is short and full of trouble, and when man comes to his end there is no remedy; no man was ever known to return from the grave.... come then, let us enjoy the good things while we can, and make full use of the creation, with all the eagerness of youth.... Down with the poor and honest man! Let us tread him under foot.... For us let might be right!"... So they argued, and very wrong they were... they never expected that holiness of life would have its recompense.... But the godless shall meet the punishment their evil thoughts deserve.... So in the day of reckoning for their sins, they will come cringing, convicted to their faces by their lawless doings.
>
> (Wisd. of Sol. 2:1, 6, 10, 21–22; 3:10a; 4:20, *NEB*)

Here a theme of the older Wisdom Literature is expanded. Through wisdom and piety one can escape not only those earthly conditions which may metaphorically be described as "death" (Proverbs 1–9), including premature biological death (Proverbs 10–31) but also the implications of mortality (Ecclesiastes). Thus death in *all* its manifestations is to be feared only by the wicked. The righteous therefore may face it with courage.

5. Death, apart from the situation of martyrdom, sometimes evokes a reluctance to depart, even fear. "Death" is sometimes depicted as a fearsome spectre in human form. Thus in the Testament of Abraham when Death is sent by God to take the patriarch's soul, it must be disguised in an attractive form:

> Abraham said to Death, "Show us your rottenness." And Death showed him rottenness, and he had two heads: the one had the face of a dragon and through it certain men die at once by asps; the other head was like a sword.... On that day Abraham's servants died because of the fear of Death.[14]
>
> (Test. of Abraham, recension B, chap. 14; first century A.D.)[15]

In a longer recension (A, perhaps slightly later in date)[16] death is described as "the common, inexorable, bitter cup" (1:10) which Abraham sought to delay by refusing to make his testament. In recognition of his righteousness the archangel Michael is sent to summon him directly to the divine presence, in contrast to all other mortals, who descend immediately to Hades at death (8:30; 19:19ff.). Not enamored at the prospect of death even under this unusual circumstance, Abraham declines the invitation and Michael returns empty-handed (chap. 7). A second summons through Michael produces the same result (chap. 9), since Abraham first desires a tour of all of creation (chaps. 10—14). Finally, Death himself is summoned, given an attractive appearance, and dispatched to summon the patriarch's soul (chap. 16). Hounded inexorably by this figure whose summons he refuses, Abraham finally asks to see him in his true form. After having been warned of the terrors which he is to behold, Abraham is shown seven dragon heads with fourteen faces—vipers, lions, lightning, sword, the chaotic sea, cups of poison, and deadly sickness—whereupon seven thousand of Abraham's servants die and Abraham himself faints away (chap. 18).

Yet the author's purpose in relating these fearsome descriptions of death is not to suggest that death is ultimately to be feared. Rather, it is the reverse. Thus he depicts Death, when first summoned before the Deity, as himself trembling with fear: "He stood before the unseen Father, trembling, moaning, and shaking, awaiting the command of the Master" (Test. of Abraham A, 16:20ff.). All autonomy is thus denied him. Furthermore, at Abraham's urging, the two of them kneel in prayer for the servants who died at Death's appearance, thus acknowledging God's sovereignty over life and death, and perhaps providing a release of tension for the hearer through this ironic scene (chap. 18). Finally, Abraham relents and his soul is taken to the divine presence (chap. 20).

That the author must labor at such length to make his point is perhaps indicative of the mentality of his intended audience. Just as the reports of the willing death of the pious martyrs were meant to encourage those "average" folk who might not be as equal to the task, so Abraham's reluctance, even fear, at a natural death after a successful life of 995 years duration, may indicate that the "average" member of the community evidenced considerable anxiety about mortality. It is a mentality totally at variance with anything in the canonical literature (which never depicts the righteous, or even the aged wicked for that matter, as evidencing such anxiety). Perhaps a reason for this mentality is concealed in the author's portrait of Death as a power or agent completely under God's sovereignty. Presumably the repressed and banished demons of antiquity, once again unleashed to prey upon the world, have in popular thought tended to gain a measure of autonomy, leaving the pious to some degree at their mercy. (This is made clear in the following section.)

6. Death in all its manifestations (metaphoric and biological) initially resulted from "the devil's spite" (Wisd. of Sol. 2:23–24). Various OT stories could now be reinterpreted so as to portray his origins and devious activity throughout history:[17] as the serpent in the Garden of Eden (Life of Adam and Eve 16 [first century A.D.]); as the leader of the "sons of God" who consort with human women in Gen. 6:1–4 (First [Ethiopic] Book of Enoch 54:6 [first century B.C.? first century A.D.?]); and as the divinely sanctioned prosecutor ("the satan") in Job 1–2 who as early as 1 Chron. 21:1 begins to be blamed for events earlier attributed to Yahweh (2 Sam. 24:1). The designation of office becomes a proper name (Satan), often rendered by the Septuagint (third to first century B.C.) as *diabolos,* "the devil" (e.g., at Job 1:6). Since this malign being was now identified with a member of the heavenly council, it was necessary to envision a rebellion prior to creation which had resulted in his expulsion along with a number of cohorts (Life of Adam and Eve 12–16).[18]

This malign being, having been granted a measure of autonomy, was responsible ultimately not only for death but also for "all man's afflictions and all their moments of tribulation" (1 QS III, 17–22).

## C. THE DEAD SEA SCROLLS

In the sectarian literature of the ascetic community at Qumran (ca. first century B.C.), biological death is scarcely an issue. The majority of the few references that do occur concern the use of the death penalty.[19] We may assume, therefore, that external persecution is not the intense problem that it is for other groups during this period, although the community was later destroyed by the Romans (late first century A.D.). Instead, attention is focused upon a this-worldly transition from one mode of existence to another: from what may be described metaphorically as "death" to "life." Such a transition, long urged in Israel's covenant formulations and in Wisdom's advice, is now tied specifically to membership in the community at Qumran. Through participation in its regimented life-style and its esoteric scriptural lore, one can escape a natural inclination toward sin, avoid the assaults of the "Angel of Darkness" who tries to mislead humans, and be in communion with the hosts of heaven. "When the sectarian enters the community, he passes from death and alienation from God to life, knowledge of God, and communion with the angels. Although a certain tension remains and he still lives in an evil world, he is nevertheless already participating in the eternal life."[20] This perspective may be detected even in several difficult and much debated passages.

> I give thanks to you, my God,
> for you have dealt marvelously with dust;[21]
> you have shown your power mightily,
>     mightily in a creature of clay.
> . . . . . . . . . . . . . . . . . . . . . . . . . . . . .
> And for the sake of your glory,
> you have cleansed man from sin, that he might be holy
> ... that he might be joined with the sons of your truth,
> and in a lot with your holy ones;[22]
> that (you) may raise up the mortal worm[23]
>     from the dust to the secret [of your truth]
>     and from a perverse spirit to [your] understanding;
> and that he may be stationed before you
>     with the everlasting host and the spirits of [        ].[24]
>                     (1 QH XI, 3, 10–13 = Hymn 17)

Rather than a description of a resurrection of the dead as some scholars have proposed,[25] we seem to have a description of God's graciousness in extending knowledge of himself to undeserving creatures. Human beings, inescapably sinners (1 QH IV, 29–30), are deserving of God's contempt. Yet through his gracious election of the community (1 QH IV, 5, 31; X, 3–4) and the revelations which accompany it, man's perverse nature is cleansed (1 QH III, 21) and his transgressions are forgiven (1 QH XVII, 15). Thus the community can share angelic insights, envision itself as even now standing with the heavenly hosts in the divine assembly,[26] and enjoy a foretaste of the "era of divine favor" (1 QH III, 21–22).

> I give thanks to you, O Lord,
> for you have redeemed me from the pit;
> and from Sheol Abaddon[27] you have lifted me up to an eternal height;
> And I walk to and fro on an unsearchable plain.[28]
> . . . . . . . . . . . . . . . . . . . . . . . . . . . . . . . . . . . . . .
> And the perverse spirit you have cleansed from great transgression to
>    be stationed with the host of the holy ones,
> And to enter into fellowship with the congregation of the children of
>    heaven.[29]
>
> (1 QH III, 10–22 = Hymn 6)

Although some scholars have seen in this passage evidence of a belief in the immortality of the soul and a hope of dwelling forever in heaven,[30] the majority of scholars see in it only another articulation of the merits of belonging to the community: one already experiences the blessings of the end-time. "Sheol" and "the Pit" are used metaphorically, as in the OT, but with the added factor that malign divine powers are arrayed against the righteous. An "eternal height" *(rum 'olam)* is used elsewhere (1 QH XV, 17; 1 QSb V, 23) to describe the benefits to be found in the community.

Given the facts that (*a*) apocalyptic eschatology, which usually includes a doctrine of life after death, is well attested in the Qumran literature;[31] (*b*) copies of apocalyptic books containing that doctrine (e.g., Daniel, Enoch) were known to the community; and (*c*) ancient writers (Josephus and Hippolytus) attribute to the Essene community (to be identified as that at Qumran by most scholars) a belief in the immortality of the soul[32]—what then is to be the fate of the righteous deceased?

The eschatology of the community includes the idea that history may be divided into a number of ages, each ending with a catastrophe induced by apostasy and each survived by a remnant which preserved the historic faith.[33] During the present age the ungodly, under the leadership of the wicked "Angel of Darkness," try to lead the righteous astray (1 QH IV, 7, 16–17). The latter are led by the "Prince of Light," and hence a cosmic battle is already under way.

At its culmination the community will participate in the struggle (as in the Book of Daniel).

> Then the sword of God will hasten at the time of judgment,
> and all the sons of his tr[u]th will awake[34] to [destroy] wickedness
> ................................................................
> Those who lie in the dust have raised a pole,
> and the wormy dead ones[35] have lifted a banner.[36]
>
> (1 QH VI, 29–34 = Hymn 10)

This passage above all others in the Qumran literature has been taken as a reference to resurrection,[37] although opinion is far from unanimous.[38] "Dwelling in dust" is often used in the OT to describe humility (1 Sam. 2:8; Ps. 44:25) and even the community in a despondent condition (Isa. 26:19).[39] Furthermore, in Hymn 17 (quoted above), being raised from the "dust" is linked with being cleansed from sin, being given understanding as a member of the community, and thereby standing with the heavenly hosts.

The wicked, in addition to punishment during this life (1 QH XIV, 24; VII, 22–23), will be "cut off" without survivor during the era of wrath (1 QS IV, 12–14). The righteous, on the other hand, will leave offspring who will survive into the era of divine favor, when the Aaronic and Davidic messiahs will preside over a renewed community centered about Jerusalem.

Whether or not the dead will be raised to participate in that era remains a topic of scholarly debate. It seems safe to conclude with Nickelsburg, however, that the published Qumran scrolls "contain not a single passage that can be interpreted with absolute certainty as a reference to resurrection or immortality." This silence is to be explained, he thinks, by the community's belief that "the decisive eschatological event has already happened." Continuity between eternal life now and in the future is so certain that there is no need to dwell upon physical death: it is inconsequential.[40]

# CHAPTER 6

# The New Testament

Several emphases of the Intertestamental literature will be continued or developed in the NT: apocalyptic eschatology, with its emphasis upon the defeat of the power of chaos, will now more explicitly include the banishing of death from human experience; resurrection will continue to be a part of the renewal of creation (and of the community) rather than an end in itself; a causal connection between sin and mortality will be more confidently asserted; "realized eschatology" (Qumran) will be expressed as participation in "eternal life" which Jesus already mediates; the etiology (or etiologies) on death in Genesis 2—3 will be more explicitly interpreted to mean that death was an intrusion into the Creator's design; "death" in all its forms (metaphor, power, biological cessation) will be united into a single force, much as may have been the case in pre-Yahwistic faith (a manifestation of the divine Mot);[1] and yet the fearfulness of death will be muted by the perception that its power has been broken by the resurrection of Jesus, who continues to empower his disciples. The tradition thus moves from the recording of aspiration to affirmation and the proclamation of confirmation.

## A. PAUL

In the thought of the earliest NT spokesman (ca. A.D. 50), and especially in the Book of Romans, death becomes a far more pervasive problem than it has been in most previous writers. His concern is more than premature death (as it was especially in such Wisdom books as Proverbs); more than such human limitations as illness, persecution, and alienation, which detract from full life in community (called "death" in Israel's covenant formulations and in the Psalms); more than mortality as a vexing problem (as it was in Ecclesiastes). Rather, it is "death" in the widest possible metaphoric sense of the term: as everything within creation which deviates from the Creator's design. As in apocalyptic eschatology, the world itself is perceived to'be in a state of decay.

Just as premature death had often previously been attributed to human error or sin, so now that explanation will be generalized to cover not only mortality (following Ecclus. 25:24) but also the deathwardness of the world (following a hint in Bk. Jub. 3:28). Furthermore, it will be stressed that "death" was first and paradigmatically manifest in the rebellion of the couple in the Garden of Eden. Thus in contrast to the OT and much of Rabbinic Judaism, Genesis 2–3 will be read so that mortality is a consequence of sin rather than the Creator's design.

> One man's trespass led to condemnation for all men. . . . by one man's disobedience many were made sinners.
>
> (Rom. 5:18–19)

> The wages of sin is death.[2]
>
> (Rom. 6:23)

> For the created universe . . . was made the victim of frustration, not by its own choice, but because of him who made it so; yet always there was hope, because the universe is to be freed from the shackles of mortality and enter into the liberty and splendor of the children of God. Up to the present, we know the whole created universe groans in all its parts as if in the pangs of childbirth.
>
> (Rom. 8:19–22, NEB)

In the last passage Paul apparently refers to the curses which God pronounced following the disobedience in Eden not merely upon the human race ("pain," "toil") but upon the earth itself (Gen. 3:16–19). Thus the entire world could be viewed as futile and death directed. "Death" is the paradigm of all existence, the background of all patterns of possibility; demoralizing, challenging, and negating all human vitality and sense of purpose.[3] A well-known hymn puts the point clearly: "change and decay in all around I see."

But death, so perceived, is more than a metaphor for less-than-ideal conditions. It is a manifestation of the power of sin related to the activity of the devil, which has infected the entire world and set it in opposition to the Creator's design. The hostile forces arrayed against the community and individual were more than human forces within and without; the greatest danger was from the higher, unseen forces with whom the earthly evil was allied.[4]

> For we are not contending against flesh and blood, but against the principalities, against the powers, against the world rulers of this present darkness, against the spiritual hosts of wickedness in the heavenly places.
>
> (Eph. 6:12)[5]

Mortality, within this larger sphere of "death," is thus not ultimately an acceptable manifestation of the Creator's will and wisdom, but an intrusion into and perversion of his will. Mortality has become an evil which ultimately will be overcome:

> For he (Christ) must reign until he has put all his enemies under his feet. The last enemy to be destroyed is death.
>
> (1 Cor. 15:25–26)

Since mortality is viewed as a historical event and problem rather than proper design (OT) or ontic flaw (Gnosticism), that is, since "Adam" has been moved from the realm of "story" to the realm of "history,"[6] mortality may now be subjected to a historical solution. Jesus, perceived as having arisen from the dead, illustrates that the resurrection hope of apocalypticism is well founded and that the transition to a new age (or world) is imminent.

> Now if Christ is preached as raised from the dead, how can some of you say that there is no resurrection of the dead? ... But in fact Christ has been raised from the dead, the first fruits of those who have fallen asleep.
>
> (1 Cor. 15:12, 20)

Thus God's victory over the forces of chaos (including death), longed for in apocalyptic eschatology, moves from the realm of poetic hope and aspiration to confirmation and affirmation. Death has been defeated, although temporarily it continues to manifest itself biologically.[7] Even that will cease at the transition to the new age, when all the followers of Jesus, living or deceased, will be granted "immortality" (1 Cor. 15:53–54).

Some of the benefits of that new age may be enjoyed in the

present, however. The perception of the implications of Jesus' resurrection now empowers his followers to act. They can perceive the world in a new light, see new patterns of possibility, "walk in newness of life" (Rom. 6:4).

Just as God's first creation included the transfer of his life-giving power ("breath") to the first *'adam,* whose actions foreshadow (anticipate?)[8] those who come after him, so God's new creation is initiated in the appearance of a new *'adam* empowered by his "spirit," whose actions empower those who come after him.

> Thus it is written, "The first Adam became a living being"; the last Adam became a life-giving spirit.... The first man was from the earth, a man of dust; the second man is from heaven. As was the man of dust, so are those who are of the dust; and as is the man of heaven, so are those who are of heaven. Just as we have borne the image of the man of dust, we shall also bear the image of the man of heaven.
>
> (1 Cor. 15:45, 47–49)

The Son is the firstborn of all creation (Col. 1:15), both the original creation (v. 16) and that now signaled by his resurrection (vv. 18–20). And his followers likewise are "a new creation" (2 Cor. 5:17; cf. Gal. 6:15).

The resurrection of the dead for Paul was not an isolated event, not merely the recreation of persons, as if that were needed to solve the problem of theodicy. Rather, it was part and parcel of the rebirth of the entire world. Within that perception of the renewal of creation, whose antecedents go back to the protoapocalypticism of the OT (e.g., Isa. 66:22), Paul's concern is a community of relatedness (an even more ancient OT idea), not a mere grave-emptying operation. (See above, p. 76.)

Paul's reaction toward biological death, and his own death in particular, is articulated as follows:

> So we are always of good courage; we know that while we are at home in the body we are away from the Lord.... we would rather be away from the body and at home with the Lord. So whether we are at home or away, we make it our aim to please him.
>
> (2 Cor. 5:6–9)

> Life to me, of course, is Christ, but then death would bring me something more; but then again, if living in this body means doing work which is having good results—I do not know what I should choose. I

am caught in this dilemma: I want to be gone and be with Christ, which would be very much better, but for me to stay alive in this world is more urgent for your sake.

(Phil. 1:21-24, *JB*)

While mortality remains a manifestation of the world's fallen state (in contrast to the OT), the timing of individual death is of some importance (in agreement with the OT). Death is not a desirable escape from the world (as in Hellenistic literature and in some of the martyr descriptions of the Intertestamental literature). As a part of the world's paradigm which is passing away, it loses its power to impel or to negate one's energies. It has lost its ultimacy.

## B. THE SYNOPTIC GOSPELS

It is difficult to recover a clear, systematic perspective on death in the writings of Matthew, Mark, and Luke, in part because they have used a number of earlier sources and in part because the topic is seldom directly addressed. Nonetheless they stand within the general framework of apocalyptic eschatology, as apparently did Jesus himself.[9] But there is little of the detailed speculation about the nature of life after death which characterizes some of the Intertestamental literature (e.g., First [Ethiopic] Book of Enoch) and to a lesser extent the NT Book of Revelation.[10] Rather, if we exclude references to Jesus' own death and to his acts of raising the dead, biological death is primarily alluded to as an incentive to prepare for the impending arrival of the new age. The insecurity and shortness of life serve to mark the narrow boundaries within which the appeals of Jesus may be heard.[11]

In those days came John the Baptist, preaching in the wilderness of Judea, "Repent, for the kingdom of heaven is at hand.... Even now the ax is laid to the root of the trees; every tree therefore that does not bear good fruit is cut down and thrown into the fire."

(Matt. 3:1-2, 10)

And he (Jesus) told them a parable, saying, "The land of a rich man brought forth plentifully....And he said, '...I will pull down my barns, and build larger ones.'...But God said to him, 'Fool! This night your soul is required of you; and the things you have prepared, whose will they be?'"

(Luke 12:16-20)

Death, then, either in a metaphoric sense or as mortality, is not presented as a paradigm of all existence (as in Paul), or even as the major problem which humans face:

> And do not fear those who kill the body but cannot kill the soul; rather, fear him (God) who can destroy both soul and body in hell.
>
> (Matt. 10:28)

This saying is given in the context of various aspects of discipleship. One must have ultimate regard for God rather than for human coercive powers, even when life is threatened. This is made clearer when the text goes on to talk about the necessity for deciding about Jesus:

> So everyone who acknowledges me before men, I also will acknowledge before my Father who is in heaven.
>
> (Matt. 10:32)

While a resurrection of the dead is assumed (e.g., Luke 14:14), it is not stressed in such fashion as to depreciate the importance of this life. It is within the present world that one is called upon to decide about and to follow Jesus, and concerning which many directives are given to his followers. There is no withdrawal from the world, in contrast to some earlier materials and to later groups within the church.

Whatever the connection between sin and mortality, or even premature death, it is not stressed and indeed at times seems to be denied.

> There were some present at that very time who told him (Jesus) of the Galileans whose blood Pilate had mingled with their sacrifices. And he answered them, "Do you think that these Galileans were worse sinners than all the other Galileans, because they suffered thus? I tell you, No; but unless you repent you will all likewise perish."
>
> (Luke 13:1–3)

> Another parable he put before them, saying, "The kingdom of heaven may be compared to a man who sowed good seed in his field; but... his enemy came and sowed weeds among the wheat, and went away. So when the plants came up and bore grain, then the weeds appeared also.... The servants said to him (the landowner), 'Then do you want us to go and gather them?' But he said, 'No; lest in gathering the weeds you root up the wheat along with them. Let them grow together until the harvest.'"
>
> (Matt. 13:24–30)

Jesus' reaction to his own impending death has been contrasted, in Cullmann's famous essay,[12] with that of the Greek philosopher Socrates. The latter believed in the innate immortality of the soul and thus, in typical Hellenistic fashion, viewed death as "the great liberator from an essentially evil world and from a limiting bodily existence." He lived his belief to the full, committing suicide with "complete peace and composure." Jesus, on the other hand, is said to have had an entirely different anthropology, which mandated a belief in resurrection. He died *totally* ("in body and soul"), and hence viewed death as a terrible destroyer, the enemy of God. In the biblical accounts, Jesus begins to "be greatly distressed and troubled" (Mark 14:33), he prays that he may be spared the ordeal which lies before him (v. 36), he does not want to be left alone (v. 37), he implores God "with loud cries and tears" (Heb. 5:7), and in his dying moment cries that God has forsaken him (Mark 15:34). This indeed seems a fitting reaction to God's great and "last enemy," as Paul puts it (1 Cor. 15:26). However, it seems to be a far more anxious response than Paul anticipates for himself. To be sure, the latter's wish to be "at home" with Christ was not uttered with crucifixion in view, and he sounds more like Socrates than like Jesus!

There are a number of problems with Cullmann's essay. Can one really depict Socrates' reaction as indicative of "the Greek philosophers," who were in reality a diverse group?[13] Can one clearly contrast "immortality" and "resurrection" in Jewish thought at the time of the NT?[14] Do the Gospels depict the "soul" as demolished by death? Whatever one's answers to these questions may be (and it seems to me that they must be in the negative), Jesus' perception of death (as an enemy of God) and his reaction to it are *not* a continuation of those of the OT (Cullmann to the contrary). They seem much closer to stances in the Intertestamental literature.

"Death" as an enemy is perceptible not only in Jesus' reaction to his impending arrest and execution but also in the proclamation that it has no place in the Kingdom which his ministry inaugurates. Not only will its effects be reversed in the resurrection, but it is linked with malign powers:

> And he called to him his twelve disciples and gave them authority over unclean spirits, to cast them out, and to heal every disease and

infirmity. . . . These twelve Jesus sent out, charging them, ". . . Heal the sick, raise the dead, cleanse lepers, cast out demons."

(Matt. 10:1, 5, 8)

Metaphoric use of the term *death* is rather rare. The best-known instance occurs in Jesus' demand that disciples follow him without delay: "Follow me, and leave the dead[15] to bury their own dead" (Matt. 8:22).

## C. THE GOSPEL OF JOHN

In this latest of the Gospels (end of the first century A.D.?) the apocalyptic theme of a catastrophic transition to a new age (including a resurrection of the dead) is pushed to the margins of discussion. It is not so much that such future transformation is denied as that God's decisive activity is perceived as having already occurred.[16] The quality of one's existence here and now is stressed rather than concentration upon a resurrection at some unknown time beyond biological death. Jesus is already present with his followers, mediating such existence:[17]

In him was life, and the life was the light of men. The light shines in the darkness, and the darkness has not overcome it.

(1:4)

He who believes in the Son has eternal life; he who does not obey the Son will never see life.

(3:36)

He who hears my words and believes him who sent me, has eternal life; he does not come into judgment, but has passed from death to life.

(5:24)

Biological death is not a fundamental problem and is seldom mentioned. Nor is it even symptomatic of the deathwardness of an entire world, which must be transformed. Rather, it is a metaphor for a quality of existence which the followers of Jesus are able to transcend. They do not participate in death-oriented existence, even though they biologically expire:

Jesus said to her, "I am the resurrection and the life; he who believes in me, though he die, yet shall he live, and whoever lives and believes in me shall never die."

(11:25–26)

Jesus' reaction to his own impending death shifts from that depicted in the synoptic Gospels. Whereas there it seems to be a fearful ordeal to be endured, now it becomes a deliberate, positive act:

> For this reason the Father loves me, because I lay down my life.... No one takes it from me, but I lay it down of my own accord. I have power to lay it down, and I have power to take it again.
>
> (10:17-18)

And whereas in Paul it is Jesus' *resurrection* that is stressed, a resurrection that is a *destruction* of the powers of sin and death, in John it is Jesus' *death* that becomes the decisive act, the means whereby his *constructive* power is unleashed to his followers.[18]

> The hour has come for the Son of man to be glorified.... unless a grain of wheat falls into the earth and dies, it remains alone; but if dies, it bears much fruit.
>
> (12:23-24)

It is in the expending of his life that Jesus unleashes a new possibility-pattern, a new paradigm of existence; it is in the vitalizing of others that one becomes truly alive. "Life" is not merely a dynamic from within: it includes the power to transform others.[19]

> We... have crossed over from death to life; we know this, because we love our brothers. The man who does not love is still in the realm of death.... It is by this that we know what love is: that Christ laid down his life for us. And we in our turn are bound to lay down our lives for our brothers.
>
> (1 John 3:14-16, *NEB*)

## D. REVELATION

Written late in the first century A.D., this apocalyptic work reflects an intense hatred of the Roman Empire because of its persecution of the saints of the church. Its major thesis seems to be that the martyrs will be vindicated through a resurrection of the dead so that they may enjoy a special reign with Christ over the earth for a period of a thousand years (20:1-6). At the same time the writer makes quite clear his belief that death is an evil instituted by the activity of the devil, who is likewise responsible for sickness and misfortune (9:1-11). The war against this cosmic force of evil begins in heaven (as earlier the Book of Daniel had depicted): after Christ receives the heavenly kingship (chap. 5), Satan is cast down to earth (chap. 12). Thereafter the followers of the Christ and of Satan struggle with each other until Christ's kingship is likewise asserted over the earth at the initiation of the millennial reign (19:11—20:6). Finally, Christ's victory extends even to the underworld: Satan, "Death," and Hades are destroyed:

> And the devil who had deceived them was thrown into the lake of fire and brimstone.
>
> (20:10)

> Then Death and Hades were thrown into the lake of fire. This is the second death.
>
> (20:14)

Then, in words reminiscent of the visions of the Book of Isaiah, "a new heaven and a new earth" are described, wherein God will dwell with his people.

> He will dwell with them, and they shall be his people, and God himself will be with them; he will wipe away every tear from their eyes, and death shall be no more, neither shall there be mourning nor crying nor pain any more, for the former things have passed away.
>
> (21:3-4)

| Concluding Reflections

## A. GENERAL OBSERVATIONS AND EVALUATION OF THE LITERATURE SURVEYED

a. It is precarious to speak of *the* biblical response to death. Rather, there is a variety of responses, depending upon the time and circumstance. Nonetheless some views tend to predominate, to endure, or to have a common denominator.

b. Since all of the responses are (at least to some extent) historically conditioned, and since all of them have been preserved (canonized) by communal decision, any one of them need not *automatically* be considered superior to the others. Since more than one stance was "normative" for its time and proved to be an effective coping mechanism, all of them may have a contribution to make to the attitudes of members of the believing communities (synagogue and church) in the present. Rather than a priori hierarchical values (such as early is authentic; latest is the fullest revelation; the NT alone is binding on the church; Jesus' perspective is ultimate), it may be that the communities' situation in the present will ultimately determine which biblical response is the most meaningful, after dialogue with the entirety of the canon.[1]

## B. POSSIBLE IMPLICATIONS FOR BIOETHICS AND THE CARE OF THE DYING[2]

The Bible, as any other document ancient or modern, is heavily dependent upon its cultural milieu, a milieu which is radically different from that of the modern Western reader.[3] This, plus the fact that biomedical technology has thrust upon us problems far beyond the imagination of the biblical theologians, makes it extremely hazardous to propose simplistic "contemporizations."[4] Nonetheless those who find their identity within the Judeo-Christian tradition cannot avoid the task.[5] For them, as well as for all those whose ultimate points of reference include the Bible, the following observations, cautions, and implications are offered.

a. The Bible contains a number of reflections upon and reactions to death. As canon it preserves a normative *range of reflection* for the community as it encounters subsequent historical ambiguities. Its pluralism is thus a strength rather than a weakness, however frustrating this may be for reaching a particular ethical decision in the present.

b. Death is more than biological cessation. It affects the human in various manifestations from the moment of birth onward. The Bible's metaphoric usages of the term correspond, roughly, to such modern perceptions as psychological death, social death, and "spiritual" death. Given ancient Israel's holistic anthropology (above, chap. 3, sec. E), the various manifestations of death unavoidably affect the total person. The accuracy of this ancient perception is now widely recognized in such disciplines as psychosomatic[6] and somatopsychic studies.[7] As illustrations of the former connection, there are statistical evidences that prolonged bereavement (especially for a mate) often leads to mental disorder, various physiological diseases (including cancer), and suicide.[8]

The training of health-care professionals must continue to be widened lest dehumanizing tendencies contribute to "death." Today's edition of the *Durham Morning Herald* contains a letter which describes a widespread though by no means universal failure in this regard.[9] It was written by a nurse with fifteen years of practical experience who left the profession because of its limitations and is now a professor of educational psychology. She describes nursing as "one of the least humane of the helping professions," in part because nurses are forbidden to give the patients innocuous although helpful information (e.g., their temperature), because safety measures are sometimes based upon protection of the institution from lawsuit rather than upon concern for the patients' well-being, because patients are stripped of their dignity in order to accommodate the hospital's routine, and because personal interaction with patients may become so minimal that they become a "thing": "I saw nurses regulate the various gadgets hanging over beds without looking at the occupants."

Counselors of the terminally ill must have a greater awareness of the manifold attack and experience of death:[10] estrangement,[11] loss of control,[12] a feeling of uselessness,[13] pain, as well as knowledge of the range, formfulness, and progression of grief.[14]

c. Life is more than biological functioning. Therefore members of the "believing communities" should always be concerned to actualize the often distinctive socioeconomic values which set Israel apart from their neighbors and which they described as life-giving. The "helping professions" must continue to be concerned with the total person in a total environment for healing.[15] Moreover, proper care for the terminally ill might include psychotherapy that enables them to grow, to "live" fully, regardless of their remaining life span. More usually therapists and physicians may categorize such patients in terms of the possibility for recovery or duration of time remaining: one assigns priority to long-term productivity or long-term relationship ("No need to waste time on patient X!"). By way of contrast,

> Perhaps life can be seen more validly as an extension in values than as an extension in time.... If a person has one hour to live and discovers himself and his life in that hour, is not this a valid and important growth? There are no deadlines on living, none on what one may do or feel so long as one is alive.[16]

The isolation of the patient, through technical apparatus, strictures on visitors, pretense that patients do not know or wish to know or discuss the seriousness of their condition, sedation, and so forth, is a denial of life-as-relatedness. It amounts to expulsion of the patient from the community and greatly strengthens the power of "death."[17]

Especially to be commended is the increasing utilization of hospice care for the terminally ill: a more homelike (though often hospital-related) environment that allows certain categories of patients to live more fully and comfortably (e.g., to move throughout the facility, to have visitors of all ages at any time, to determine the amount of medication needed for control of pain).[18]

d. The Bible does not stress the idea that human life is so intrinsically sacred that it must be preserved at *all* costs. For example, it could be taken in battle or in a socially sanctioned execution.[19] This reality, coupled with the aforementioned principle that life is more than mere biological functioning (shall we therefore continue to treat the body when the larger whole person has died?), *could* be seen as compatible with a modern stance that would allow extraordinary life-support systems to be withdrawn from some categories of dying patients. However, several cautions, perhaps even counter-indications, would seem to be in order. *(a)* The power of life is envisioned as belonging intrinsically to the Deity, and it is given to creatures only through a special creative act (Gen. 2:7; Ps. 104:30). *(b)* The power to procreate (to extend the Creator's life-giving power) is regarded as a special blessing (Gen. 1:28; 8:17)[20] *(c)* The taking of human life (save under the conditions specified above) is such an arrogant usurpation of power that execution must result. The offense is not basically against another human, it is against the Deity:

> Whoever sheds the blood of a man, by man shall his blood be shed; for God made man in his own image.
>
> (Gen. 9:6)

Thus if life does not have such absolute value as to forbid execution, at least execution is perceived as the only fitting penalty for violating its sanctity. *(d)* Even a beast must not be allowed to deprive a human being of life without forfeiting its own in return (Gen. 9:5). *(e)* Blood, thought to contain the life-force, is forbidden as a food ingredient. This prohibition is of such importance that it is repeated six times in the Pentateuch (e.g., Gen. 9:4). *(f)* The (profane) slaughter of domestic food-animals is forbidden. Even their life cannot be terminated without the enactment of a ritual which acknowledges God's sovereignty over it (Lev. 17:1–16). Otherwise the action is to be categorized as murder and appropriate sanctions are to be taken:

> Bloodguilt shall be imputed to that man; he has shed blood; and that man shall be cut off from among his people.
>
> (Lev. 17:4)

Thus the sanctity of life, while not absolute, is so surrounded with barriers against violation that any contemporary attempt to sanction the withholding or withdrawing of life-support systems from terminally ill patients cannot appeal monolithically to the Bible for support. Perhaps the most that can be said is that the issue is an ambiguous one, and that the Bible is an accurate reflection of the ambiguity.

e. Physicians who tend to view death as a challenge to their ability, as an "opponent" to be overcome at all costs, will feel more kinship with the predominant stance of the NT (death as an evil "power" which God will soon eradicate) than they will with that of the OT (death as a natural event).

f. Since the biblical mentality cannot conceive of existence in non-corporeal terms and thus forbade desecration of corpses or even of bones, modern orthodox Judaism quite logically has opposed autopsies and cremation as sacrilege.[21] The mentality contained in the often-heard modern statement, "Do with my corpse as you please, since it is no longer me," is entirely alien to that of ancient Israel, and perhaps to early Christianity as well.

g. The expectation of life after death may only with difficulty become a factor in ethical decisions. In the biblical text itself, it is not used to devalue this-worldly existence.

## C. RELIGION AND THE FEAR OF DEATH[22]

In chaps. 2–3 I have suggested, based upon the available evidence, that the Yahwists of ancient Israel seem to have been less anxious about mortality than were their neighbors. But what of their spiritual descendants in the present? Do contemporary Christians and Jews cope with death more effectively than other persons in our society?

In recent years a number of social scientists have investigated the relationship between religious belief and attitude toward death.[23] Thus far the results have been inconclusive or contradictory. Herman Feifel, for example, surveying eighty-four persons of middle age, concluded that "the religious person, when compared with the nonreligious individual, is personally more afraid of death."[24] Irving Alexander and Arthur Adlerstein, testing fifty undergraduate males at Princeton, decided that both "religious and nonreligious" subjects have comparable negative feelings about death.[25] In another report on the same investigation, they suggested that each group had reduced anxiety in its own way and with about equal success:

the former by believing in an afterlife and the latter by repression of thought about dying.[26] David Martin and Lawrence Wrightsman, studying fifty-eight adults of all ages who attended three small churches in Tennessee, found that religious *attitude* had no effect upon one's concern over death, but that religious *practice* reduced fear in this area.[27]

Because of the smallness and homogeneity of the groups thus far investigated, no safe generalizations can be drawn concerning the population as a whole. Even more caution should be observed when one realizes some of the methodological problems of the research. In most cases there has been no distinction between fear of death, death anxiety, and death phobia.[28] Similarly there has been a failure to distinguish fear of what happens after death, fear of the process of dying, and fear of the loss of life (mastery, separation, incompleteness).[29] How successfully have the subjects repressed the emotional provocations which the tests presented?[30] Can accurate determinations be made apart from conversations with and observations of dying patients as opposed to the use of questionnaires with persons for whom death is only a theoretical possibility?

Past researches seem to have assumed that belief in life after death is central to Judeo-Christianity, and they have focused their energies upon evaluation of it as a coping mechanism. For example, Alexander and Adlerstein structured their entire project around this concept: "The belief in an afterlife concept was employed as an absolute point of differentiation between the groups."[31] While such a criterion is logical given the centrality of that doctrine in the history of Christianity, it leaves a number of questions unanswered. Why do some firm believers in this doctrine approach death with great calmness, even anticipation, while others react with terror?[32] And what is it about life after death that relieves fear of death? The preservation of the "self"? Reunion with family and friends? Assurance of justice in the universe? To the extent that the average believer differentiates in such fashion, which belief is more effective: resurrection or immortality (without resurrection, i.e., dwelling in heaven)?

By defining the "religious" person in terms of this belief, all possibility of evaluating other resources within the biblical tradition for coping with death have been foreclosed. Does the modern Christian's increasing inability to accept the idea of an afterlife need *necessarily* engender an inability to face death?[33] Given the range of perceptions and coping mechanisms which the Bible contains, and in view of ancient Israel's apparent success in this area apart from any expectation of a meaningful afterlife, members of the believing communities in the present might do well to take seriously the entire range of canonical responses or perspectives.

At the same time it must be admitted that the modern situation has introduced stress-inducing factors that were largely unknown in ancient Israel.[34] For example, urbanization in the OT period was not so developed that the average person saw only human activity and thus had forgotten the majesty and diversity of nature; humans had not yet developed technologically such that they became intoxicated with their abilities and viewed the world only as a tool to be used for their comfort and pleasure;[35] they did not yet view the world in terms of evolution from "lower" to "higher" forms of life, so that humans could become the goal of creation.

It is in the Book of Job that the human place within the larger scheme of things is most realistically laid out. When Job protests that he is not receiving justice (to his tastes), he is reminded of the range of God's concerns: mountain goats, wild asses and oxen, the ostrich, and birds of prey (chap. 39). These animals seem to have been selected for mention because they are remote from human observation and value. Yet God has created them and enjoys them as he does humans. Hence to view the world anthropocentrically may be seen as a narrow, prideful, ignorant distortion of the divine perspective.[36]

Among modern writers, Bertrand Russell has most pointedly questioned a theology of creation which centers around human beings. Are they the most beautiful creature? The most benign to their fellows? The strongest? (Not when compared with the lowly ant!) The best adjusted to the world in which they find themselves? It might be debated, in view of the nuclear and ecological crisis which they have brought upon themselves, that they are the most intelligent. And thus he concludes: "If I were granted omnipotence, and millions of years to experiment in, I should not think Man much to boast of as the final result of all my efforts."[37]

Biblical persons, then, had less delusions of grandeur than do modern ones, were more able to see themselves with the larger scheme of creation, acknowledged an infinite chasm between themselves and the Creator ("you are clay," Gen. 3: 19),[38] and thus saw death as natural and acceptable with an ease that modern persons cannot.

## D. THE DEATHWARDNESS OF THE WORLD

Given successive and brutal invasions from without,[39] internal strife,[40] and tyrannical local administrations,[41] it is not surprising that some persons toward the end of the biblical period began to see a uniting pattern behind all of the particulars.[42] It is not so much that there are deaths as that death can be seen as an all-embracing structure. It can be seen as the manifestation of a power which negates every human possibility and renders life ultimately meaningless. And thus St. Paul can speak of the entire creation as subjected to futility and decay (Rom. 8:20-21).

Similar negating paradigms may be found in other writers, ancient or modern. Thus Bertrand Russell, reflecting upon the fact that the sun will eventually consume its fuel, remarks:

> Some day, the sun will grow cold, and life on earth will cease. The whole epoch of animals and plants is only an interlude between ages that were too hot and ages that will be too cold. There is no law of cosmic progress, but only an oscillation upward and downward, with a slow trend downward on the balance owing to the diffusion of energy. This, at least, is what science at present regards as most probable, and in our disillusioned generation it is easy to believe. From evolution, so far as our present knowledge shows, no ultimately optimistic philosophy can be validly inferred.[43]

The point at which a negating paradigm may be perceived is much closer at hand in Ernest Becker's description of creation:

> What are we to make of a creation in which the routine activity is for organisms to be tearing others apart with teeth of all types—biting, grinding flesh, plant stalks, bones between molars, pushing the pulp greedily down the gullet with delight, incorporating its essence into one's own organization, and then excreting with foul stench and gasses the residue.... not to mention the daily dismemberment and slaughter in "natural" accidents of all types: an earthquake buries alive seventy thousand bodies in Peru.... The soberest conclusion that we could make about what has actually been taking place on the planet for about three billion years is that it is being turned into a vast pit of fertilizer.

The paradigm is not always perceived, however, or at least humans are able to repress its implication, because

> the sun distracts our attention, always baking the blood dry, making things grow over it, and with its warmth giving the hope that comes with the organism's comfort and expansiveness.[44]

Jean-Paul Sartre, in rejecting Martin Heidegger's idea that anticipation and acceptance of death may serve a positive function when they become incentives to maximize the present,[45] points out that the moment of death, rather than being fittingly chosen, is almost entirely a matter of chance. It usually either leaves tasks unfinished and potentials unrealized, or it delays until accomplishments are undone.

> Thus this perpetual appearance of chance at the heart of my projects cannot be apprehended as my possibility but, on the contrary, as the nihilation of all my possibilities.... Thus death is never that which gives life its meanings; it is, on the contrary, that which on principle removes all meaning from life.[46]

Hans Morgenthau speaks of biological death as "the great scandal" which negates all human experiences. He points out that some modern persons have sought to escape its negation through the immortality of the world which they leave behind: works of art, philanthropic activity, offspring, ongoing organizations (social, political, religious). All such activity must now be perceived as futile in view of "nuclear death": we face the possibility of the destruction of all life, and with it all value.

> To defend freedom and civilization is absurd when to defend them amounts to destroying them. To die with honor is absurd if nobody is left to honor the dead. The very conception of honor and shame require a society that knows what honor and shame mean.[47]

When death is seen as the pattern of all existence, then the only hopes for meaningful existence lie in repressing that realization or in a competing paradigm which negates it.[48] For St. Paul, as we have seen (chap. 6, sec. A), such a counterparadigm was instituted through the resurrection of Jesus, which marked the destruction of the old order and unleashed new patterns of possibility.

For many modern persons an essential part of the biblical paradigm has become the survival of the "self." At a time when ability to believe in that doctrine is on the wane, even among members of the believing communities (see above, sec. C), it might be helpful to remember other perspectives within the tradition.[49] While the theologians of ancient Israel could not have imagined the total destructive power now within humans' hands and hence the crisis of meaning which "nuclear death" has thrust upon us, some of them do suggest that one's identity may be found in something more enduring than any aspect of Israel's historical destiny or the survival of offspring or the survival of the self. Thus the Book of Habakkuk closes with the articulation of a hypothetical collapse of the realm of nature. What might one's response be when the world is on the verge of reverting to the chaos of creation?[50]

> Although the fig-tree does not burgeon,
> the vines bear no fruit,
> the olive-crop fails,
> the orchards yield no food,
> the fold is bereft of its flock
> and there are no cattle in the stalls,
> yet I will exult in the Lord.
>             (3:17–18, *NEB*)

One may rejoice, even though the world itself has ceased to give life. And amidst a savage invasion by the Babylonians which brings death, the collapse of economic, social, and political structures, and which raises acutely the question of theodicy, one may still proclaim, apparently with comfort:

> Are you not from everlasting, O Lord my God, my Holy One? *You* will not die.[51]
>             (1:12, trans. and emphasis mine)

Or is that, after all, the ultimate rationalization?

## E. THE LITURGICAL RESPONSE TO DEATH

Ancient Israel's liturgical materials (foremost among which are the psalms) allowed for the expression of a wide range of human emotion: not merely affirmation and joy but doubt, fear, and even hostility. The liturgy not only acknowledged the reality of such emotions but sanctioned their expression in community: defined their limits, gave them form, and guided them in meaningful direc-

tions (see above, chap. 3, sec. F). While none of the psalms are funeral liturgies, they are concerned with the various manifestations of
"death" and rarely even with mortality (e.g., Ps. 90).

Modern liturgical debate about the function of the funeral tends
to contrast psychological concerns (grief therapy for the living) with
theological ones (e.g., the recitation of the community's kerygma).[52]
Recently the emphasis has begun to shift from the former to the
latter, as perhaps it should. Nonetheless, two observations must be
made about the emerging shape of the liturgy.

First, from a canonical point of view, the kerygma which is pro-
claimed is often quite narrow. Rather than including the wealth of
perspectives and insights which the tradition contains, the focus is
usually upon assertion of the presence of the resurrected Jesus, victory
over sin and death, eternal life now, and the "promise of preservation
of personal identity in fellowship with God and with other persons."[53]

Second, the emotional crisis of the bereaved is acknowledged (?)
and channeled only obliquely through such acts as confession of sin,
assertion of faith, and prayers of dedication.[54]

In the United Methodist Church's "Order for the Burial of the
Dead,"[55] the service opens with sentences from Scripture, the first
being, "I am the resurrection...whoever...believes in me shall
never die" (John 11:25);[56] then come comforting prayers stressing
the need for trust in God; various selections from the psalms, stressing security;[57] NT readings stressing life after death, the first being,
"Let not your heart be troubled....In my Father's house are many
mansions" (John 14:1-2); then comes the possibility of including a
hymn or anthem; then concluding prayers, including the absolute
assurance that the deceased "is at home in thy presence."

While the emotional needs of the bereaved perhaps should not be
the controlling factor in the shape of the liturgy, it might be argued
that they should receive more attention than the previous structure
allows. Not only is the overt expression of grief psychologically and
physiologically beneficial,[58] but also until it is done the worshiper
may not feel that the liturgy is true to experience. Thus a mother
whose child was dying of cancer, when advised that a visit to the
hospital chapel might be helpful, responded: "Who needs a chapel?
I need just the opposite. I need to scream and rage and curse."[59]

Moreover, if the bereaved feel that their expressions of grief are inappropriate in public (i.e., if the liturgy accommodates itself to our death-denying culture), then they tend to be isolated from the community-at-worship. The community has refused to acknowledge, define, or direct grief; it has refused to make the family's loss into "our" loss. "Community" has ceased to be.

It is not my task here, nor is it within my ability, to indicate what the specific shape of a more adequate liturgical response to death might be. It is rather to point out the jarring contrast between the realism with which some of the psalms begin, on the one hand, and the kerygmatic statements of modern liturgies during which "the bereaved seems constrained to simulate a joy which he can scarcely feel,"[60] on the other. Consider the following specimens of the former approach:

> My God, my God, why hast thou forsaken me?
> Why art thou so far from helping me, from the words of my groaning?
> O my God, I cry by day, but thou dost not answer;
>    and by night, but find no rest.
> ...........................
> I am poured out like water,
>    and all my bones are out of joint;
> my heart is like wax,
>    it is melted within my breast;
> my strength is dried up like a potsherd,
>    and my tongue cleaves to my jaws;
>    thou dost lay me in the dust of death.
>
>                          (Ps. 22:1–2, 14–15)

> Hear my prayer, O Lord;
>    let my cry come to thee!
> Do not hide thy face from me
>    in the day of my distress!
> ........................
> For my days pass away like smoke,
>    and my bones burn like a furnace.
> My heart is smitten like grass, and withered;
>    I forget to eat my bread.
>              (Ps. 102:1–4)

In any case, it appears that grief was more constructively managed in ancient Israel than it is by those in the church at present.

## F. BIOLOGICAL, PSYCHOLOGICAL, AND
## THEOLOGICAL MATURITY

From the point of view of ancient Israel's canonical faith, death is the natural consummation of biological life. Rather than a dismal interruption of life in old age, mortality is the proper boundary for creaturely existence. It has been programmed into human biology from the beginning of creation and is evident in each life from the moment of birth. St. Augustine puts it succinctly:

> As when medical men examine an illness, and ascertain that it is fatal, they make this pronouncement, "He will die, he will not get over this," so from the moment of a man's birth, it may be said, "He will not get over this."
>
> (Sermon 47, 3; *NPNF* VI:412)

> Furthermore, if every man begins to die, that is, is in death, as soon as death has begun to show itself in him...then he begins to die as soon as he begins to live.
>
> (City of God, 13.10; *NPNF* II:249)

This physiological reality ordinarily manifests itself in a parabolic curve. The infant matures slowly; the zenith of physical and mental power is reached around the age of twenty; then begins a slow decline toward the state of rest with which life began.

One's psychological development usually lags behind the physiological one. For example, we may cling to childish attitudes and values even after we have reached physiological maturity; we may not be able to admit that we have passed the zenith of physical powers and thus refuse to "act our age" (thus the "hip" septuagenarian); and the elderly often retreat to the memories of childhood. We thus detach ourselves from our physiology and refuse to accept our wholeness: "Our psychology then loses its natural basis."[61]

The individual's *theological* development may similarly be out of step with biological reality. For example, one may not be able to admit that mortality *is* the general human condition or that it is *God's* intention for his creatures or that such an intention is justified. But to be a whole person and theologically mature is to bring the three developmental curves (physiological, psychological, and theological) into phase: to accept mortality, to surrender one's life freely to the

Sovereign of life and death. Therefore death becomes more than a biological event. It may be the occasion for one's boldest act, the ultimate renunciation of egocentricity in favor of theocentricity.[62]

Such a moment of decision, the final manifestation of freedom just at the very time when one is helpless in view of inexorable death, is ultimately grounded in the faith of ancient Israel. It need not presuppose the affirmation of life after death, although it is compatible with it. It is rather a fundamental theological perspective which underlies both Testaments.

The possibility of such a decision is not limited to those who are conscious as death approaches, such that the comatose and the victim of sudden death are deprived of it. On the contrary, one may reflect upon the problem well in advance, and in such cases theological maturity will have better kept pace with physiological reality. It is the task of the clergy to encourage such maturation through regular communal reflection upon life and death in canonical perspective(s) while the inevitable final decision is still some distance away. The more usual funeral meditations, through which we may assume that we are meeting our obligations in this regard, are simply inadequate. A theology of dying is thus distinguishable from a theology of death.[63]

# Notes

CHAPTER 1. THE MODERN SITUATION

1. Leo Tolstoy, *The Death of Ivan Ilych* (New York: Signet paperback, 1960), p. 132.

2. Such anxiety-reducing designations as *grief therapist* (undertaker), *preneed memorial estate* (grave-plot), *loved one* (corpse) have often been discussed. Convenient collections may be found in Jessica Mitford, *The American Way of Death* (Greenwich: Fawcett Publications, 1963), at pp. 15–16, 62–63, 182–84.

3. "I cannot recollect a novel or play of the last twenty years or so which has a 'death-bed scene' in it, describing in any detail the death 'from natural causes' of a major character; this topic was a set piece for most of the eminent Victorian or Edwardian writers, evoking their finest prose and their most elaborate technical effects to produce the greatest amount of pathos or edification." Geoffrey Gorer, "The Pornography of Death," in his volume *Death, Grief and Mourning in Contemporary Britain* (London: Cresset Press, 1965), p. 172.

4. In general see Mitford, *American Way of Death;* more briefly David Dempsey, *The Way We Die* (New York: Macmillan Co., 1975), chap. 8 ("Bury the Death?").

5. See below, chap. 7, sec. B, for brief illustrations from the medical profession. For painful although often accurate characterizations of pastoral evasiveness see Denis McBride, "Immortality, Old Age and Death," *Review for Religious* 37 (1978): 717–29. For example: "The priest rushes in where angels fear to tread. With a finger wet with oil, he finds a space, makes a few familiar incantations, and,

with an apologetic look, bows out of the scene to take refuge in the darkness of the night from which he came. The patient gets the tranquilizer; the priest, the tranquility" (p. 724). Robert Neale has also pointed out that Scripture reading and prayer may be used by the anxious minister as a means of evasion. When people begin to be candid in their conversation, the clergy may cut them short with "Let us pray." See Neale, *The Art of Dying* (New York: Harper & Row, Publishers, 1973), pp. 12–13.

6. This position is put forth optimistically by Alan Harrington, *The Immortalist* (New York: Random House, 1969). For example: "Death is an imposition on the human race, and no longer acceptable.... [man] must now proceed physically to overcome it. In short, to kill death: to put an end to his own mortality as a certain consequence of being born" (p. 3). For a review of the cryonic approach see Dempsey, *The Way We Die,* pp. 189–91.

7. For a general survey and analysis see Walter Kaufmann, *Existentialism, Religion, and Death* (New York: Meridian Books, 1976).

8. See below, chap. 7, sec. E, for illustrations.

9. See Ernest Becker, *The Denial of Death* (New York: Macmillan Co., Free Press, 1973), chaps. 3–4, for a clear presentation of this idea.

10. Sigmund Freud, *Gesammelte Schriften,* (Leipzig: Internationaler Psycholoanalytischer Verlag), 5:332–33 (from the essay "Our Relation to Death"), as quoted by Walter Kaufmann, "Existentialism and Death," in *The Meaning of Death,* ed. Herman Feifel (New York: McGraw-Hill Book Co., 1959), p. 48. Emphasis mine.

11. Elizabeth Kübler-Ross, *On Death and Dying* (New York: Macmillan Co., 1969), p. 4. Emphasis mine. See also p. 37: "Since in our unconscious mind we are all immortal, it is almost inconceivable for us to acknowledge that we too have to face death."

12. For brief citation of medieval evidence see below. In general see Arnold Toynbee, "Traditional Attitudes toward Death," in *Man's Concern with Death,* ed. Toynbee (New York: McGraw-Hill Book Co., 1968), pp. 59–94; Jacques Choron, *Death and Western Thought* (New York: Macmillan Co., Collier Books, 1963).

13. For a discussion of the difficulty of such projection see R. W. Brockway, "Neanderthal 'Religion,'" *Studies in Religion/Sciences Religieuses,* 7 (1978): 317–21.

14. Sigmund Freud, *The Future of an Illusion* (Garden City: Doubleday Anchor Books, 1964). Initially published in 1927.

15. Such misperception (or is it denial?) might have been nurtured by the limited life span of persons in ancient times, for whom death usually came by the age of twenty. See John Hick, *Death and Eternal Life* (New York: Harper & Row, Publishers, 1976), pp. 55–58, and the sources cited there.

16. Ibid., p. 57.

17. For a brief discussion of evidence that human cells seem programmed to reproduce themselves only a limited number of times (about fifty) see Dempsey, *The Way We Die*, pp. 44–46.

18. For the psychoanalytic perspective see Becker, *The Denial of Death;* for sociological research which tends to support it see below, chap. 7, sec. C.

19. For a brief though sharp and telling analysis see Kaufmann, *Existentialism, Religion, and Death*, chap. 12 ("On Death and Lying"). He examines the various case histories presented by Kübler-Ross *(On Death and Dying)* and suggests that some of them contradict her sweeping, dogmatic assertion that "the fear of death is a universal fear."

20. See especially Toynbee, "Changing Attitudes toward Death in the Modern Western World," in *Man's Concern with Death*, pp. 122–32.

21. For the "immortalist" position see above, n. 6. Toynbee (*Man's Concern with Death*, p. 131) has suggested that citizens of the United States experience an added dimension of this mentality: death is "un-American" because it defies Yankee ingenuity, it challenges our confidence that every problem has a solution if one tries hard enough, and it undermines the "American way of life."

22. On [the] average today it takes ten to fifteen years before a member of the family dies. This means that in our time a person must be fifty before he experiences the same number of deaths as a twenty-year-old in 1820." Johann Hofmeier, "The Present-Day Experience of Death," in *The Experience of Dying*, Concilium 94 (New York: Herder & Herder, 1974), p. 15, n. 1 (citing the research of Alois Hahn).

23. The best-known and articulate critic of contemporary funeral practice is Mitford, *American Way of Death*.

24. Hofmeier, Concilium 94, p. 18.

25. A brief introduction may be found in Richard Cavendish, *Visions of Heaven and Hell* (New York: Crown Publishers, Harmony Books, 1977).

26. This desire is best attested in the *ars moriendi* literature, which continued well into the period of English Protestantism. See Mary Catharine O'Connor, *The Art of Dying Well: The Development of the Ars Moriendi* (New York: Columbia University Press, 1942); for English Protestantism see Nancy Lee Beaty, *The Craft of Dying* (New Haven: Yale University Press, 1970). The Anglican prayer book continues this mentality: "from sudden death, Lord, deliver us."

27. Antecedents of such vivid depictions likely include those to be found in Greek and Roman literature, for example, Virgil's *Aeneid* (late first century B.C.). Understandably, it is Virgil whom Dante depicts as his guide through the infernal realm in his *Divine Comedy* (fourteenth century A.D.).

28. For sociological surveys see chap. 7, sec. C, below. In general see Toynbee, *Man's Concern with Death,* pp. 130–32.

29. For ancient perceptions of the deathwardness of the world see chap. 6, sec. A, below. For the modern situation see Sam Keen, "Hope in a Posthuman Era," in *New Theology No. 5,* ed. Martin E. Marty and Dean G. Peerman (New York: Macmillan Co., 1968), pp. 79–89. Note should be made of Paul Tillich's contrary suggestion that meaninglessness has replaced death as the predominate cause of anxiety in the modern world, in *The Courage To Be* (New Haven: Yale University Press, 1952), p. 57.

30. See Paul Ramsey, "The Indignity of 'Death with Dignity,'" in *Hastings Center Studies,* 2, no. 2 (May 1974), pp. 53–54, who cites sociological surveys in n. 14. The modern preference, especially in the United States, may have been nourished by the "frontier mentality": the desire to die "with one's boots on."

31. "Death, Theology of," in IDBS.

32. For the dialectal relationship between the terms *Scripture* and *church* see David H. Kelsey, *The Uses of Scripture in Recent Theology* (Philadelphia: Fortress Press, 1975), chap. V.

33. See especially James A. Sanders, "Adaptable to Life: the Nature and Function of Canon," in *Magnalia Dei,* ed. Frank M. Cross et al. (Garden City: Doubleday & Co., 1976), pp. 531–60.

CHAPTER 2. SOME PERSPECTIVES ON DEATH
AMONG ISRAEL'S NEIGHBORS

1. *ANET,* pp. 104–6, plus Supp. Vol., pp. 512–14, for a fragmentary version. Recently published with new fragments by Wilfred Lambert and A. R. Millard, *Atra-hasis* (Oxford: University Press, 1969). For helpful reconstruction and discussion see Anne Kilmer, "The Mesopotamian Concept of Overpopulation and Its Solution as Reflected in the Mythology," *Orientalia* 41 (1972): 160–77; Tikva Frymer-Kensky, "The Atrahasis Epic and its Significance for Our Understanding of Genesis 1–9," *BA* 40 (1977): 147–55.

2. There is a distant echo of this in the Genesis creation account: the human was created in order to "till and keep" Yahweh's garden (2:15).

3. There is a distant echo of this also in the Genesis creation account: Yahweh forms the human from the "dust [clay] of the ground" and breathes into him an animating breath (2:7).

4. Although our copies come from the first millennium B.C., it is likely that the epic itself comes from the late second millennium.

5. *ANET,* pp. 60–72, plus Supp. Vol., pp. 501–3; the translation above is from Thorkild Jacobsen, *The Treasures of Darkness* (New Haven: Yale University Press, 1976), pp. 180–81.

6. OB, X.iii.1–5 (see *ANET,* p. 90).

7. For translation see *ANET,* pp. 72–99; for recent discussion of its origin, composition, and meaning, see Jacobsen, *Treasures,* chap. 7.

8. There is an echo of this etiological narrative in Genesis 3, where a snake prods humans into losing access to the "tree of life." For this type of literature see chap. 3, n. 67.

9. For discussion of the various complexes which make up the Inanna-Dumuzi story see Jacobsen, *Treasures,* chap. 2.

10. For discussion of a north Syrian magical text (seventh century B.C.) showing a demon or protective deity wielding an ax see Theodor H. Gaster, "A Canaanite Magical Text," *Orientalia,* n.s. 11 (1942): 79, fig. 1.

11. Quoted from Samuel Noah Kramer, "Cuneiform Studies and the History of Literature: The Sumerian Sacred Marriage Texts," *PAPS* 107 (1963): 493, ll. 14–21.

12. UG 5.1 (RS 24.258), ll. 15–22, as translated by Marvin Pope, *Song of Songs* (AB, 7C; Garden City: Doubleday & Co., 1977), p. 211. For full discussion see idem, "A Divine Banquet at Ugarit," in *The Use of the Old Testament in the New and Other Essays,* ed. J. M. Efird (Durham: Duke University Press, 1972), pp. 170–203.

13. See, e.g., *ERE* 4:568–71, "Demons and Spirits (Assyr.-Bab.)," by R. Campbell Thompson. The same author has treated the topic at great length in his *Devils and Evil Spirits of Babylonia,* 2 vols. (London: Luzac & Co., 1904–5). For additional treatment see *Génies, anges et Démons,* Sources orientales 8 (Paris: Éditions du Seuil, 1971), pp. 85–112 ("Anges et Démons en Babylonie"); *Le Jugement des Morts,* Sources Orientales 4 (Paris: Éditions du Seuil, 1961), pp. 81–102 ("Le Jugement des morts chez les Assyro-Babyloniens").

14. On the significance of this number among the Semites and as a designation of a specific group of demons see Hildegard and Julius Lewy, "The Origin of the Week and the Oldest West Asiatic Calendar," *HUCA* 17 (1942–43): 1–152, esp. secs. II–III.

15. Based upon *CAD,* G, pp. 18–19.

16. *CAD,* A, pp. 325–26.

17. *CAD,* A, pp. 375–77.

18. For a brief discussion and plaque see Erle Lichty, "Demons and Population Control," *Expedition* 13, no. 2 (Winter 1971): 22–26. See also *CAD,* L, 66–67.

19. *CAD,* A¹, pp. 185–86.

20. *CAD,* L, pp. 16–17.

21. Tablet IV, col. ii, ll. 14–26 of the series *utukki limnuti* ("the evil spirits"), trans. Thompson, *Devils and Evil Spirits,* 1:35.

22. See Lichty, "Demons and Population Control," for picture and brief discussion; *ANET,* Supp. Vol., fig. 857; Morris Jastrow, *Aspects of Religious Belief and Practice in Babylonia and Assyria* (Putnam's, 1911), p. 309, pl. 25, fig. 1. A collection of pictures may conveniently be found in Henry Sigerist, *Primitive and Archaic Medicine* (Oxford Press Galaxy Books, 1967).

23. Generally, see *CAD,* E, pp. 397–401.

24. "Descent of Ishtar to the Nether World," *ANET,* p. 107.

25. Gilgamesh Epic, XII. 150ff.; *ANET,* p. 99.

26. Tablet IV, col. iv, l. 40–col. vi, l. 4, *utukki limnuti,* Thompson,

*Devils and Evil Spirits,* 1:39-45. Several translation problems are given in his footnote.

27. Generally, see Miranda Bayliss, "The Cult of Dead Kin in Assyria and Babylonia," *Iraq* 35 (1973): 115-25. For Semitic and Greco-Roman mortuary cults see Marvin Pope, *Song of Songs,* AB, pp. 210-29. For late Roman practice see F. van der Meer, *Augustine the Bishop* (London: Sheed & Ward, 1961), chap. 18.

28. As quoted in Bayliss, "Cult of Dead Kin," p. 117.

29. *CAD,* A², pp. 241-42.

30. Thompson in *ERE,* 4:570-71; idem, *Devils and Evil Spirits,* 1:xxxvii-xxxviii. For a text in translation see Charles Isbell, "The Story of the Aramaic Incantation Bowls," *BA* 41 (1978): 11.

31. *CAD,* L, p. 190.

32. For a picture see Ilse Seibert, *Woman in the Ancient Near East* (Edition Leipzig, 1974), pl. 30.

33. For general discussion, Gaster, "Canaanite Magical Text."

34. Ibid.; briefly, Lichty, "Demons and Population Control."

35. Lichty, "Demons and Population Control," with photos of excavated specimens.

36. Ibid.

37. For details of prognosis, diagnosis, and treatment see Edith Ritter, "Magical-Expert ( = ašĭpu) and Physician ( = asû): Notes on Two Complementary Professions in Babylonian Medicine," *Studies in Honor of Benno Landsberger,* Assyriological Studies 16 (Chicago: University of Chicago Press, 1965), pp. 299-321. See also the individual articles in *CAD,* A², pp. 344-47, 431-35. At a popular level see Sigerist, *Primitive and Archaic Medicine,* sec. IV. 5.

38. Texts cited in Ritter, "Magical-Expert and Physician," pp. 305-6.

39. Cited in Lichty, "Demons and Population Control," p. 25. For another specimen see above under discussion of *eṭemmu,* and in general Thompson, *Devils and Evil Spirits.*

40. Cited in Ritter, "Magical-Expert and Physician," p. 311.

41. Ibid., p. 307.

42. Ibid., pp. 311-12.

43. Tablet I, ll. 352-55. For discussion of their meaning see Kilmer, "Mesopotamian Concept of Overpopulation," *Orientalia* 41

(1972): 160–77; Frymer-Kensky, "Atrahasis Epic"; and briefly, Lichty, "Demons and Population Control."

44. Far more familiar is the version found in Gilgamesh XI, wherein the flood survivors are granted immortality. See *ANET*, p. 95. See Kilmer, "Mesopotamian Concept of Overpopulation," for the above reconstruction of the older Atrahasis Epic.

45. For discussion of the effects of Mesopotamian geography upon religion see Henri Frankfort et al., *Before Philosophy: The Intellectual Adventure of Ancient Man* (Baltimore: Penguin Books, nd). For a reconstruction of the various stages ("concerns") through which Mesopotamian religion moved from the fourth to the second millennium (famine, the sword, guilt) see Jacobsen, "Ancient Mesopotamian Religion: The Central Concerns," *PAPS* 107 (1963): 473–84; and more briefly his essay "Formative Tendencies in Sumerian Religion," in *The Bible and the Ancient Near East*, ed. G. Ernest Wright (Garden City: Doubleday & Co., Anchor Books, 1965), pp. 353–68.

46. For this group of gods see Lewy and Lewy, "The Origin of the Week."

47. For the general outline see Jacobsen, *Treasures*, pp. 227–28; for this god in general, J. J. M. Roberts, "Erra—Scorched Earth," *JCS* 24 (1971): 11–16.

48. Contrast the futile and powerless requests of the lunar goddess Ningal that her city, Ur, not be destroyed. *ANET*, pp. 455–63.

49. See, e.g., "Man and his God," by Samuel Noah Kramer, *SVT* 5, pp. 170–82.

50. See esp. W. O. E. Oesterley, "Persian Angelology and Demonology," in *Occident and Orient* (Gaster Anniversary Volume), ed. Bruno Schindler (London: Taylor's Foreign Press, 1936), pp. 457–66.

51. Adapted from the translation in *ANET*, Supp. Vol., p. 658; for a slightly different translation and full commentary see Gaster, "Canaanite Magical Text."

52. William Culican, "Phoenician Demons," *JNES* 35 (1976): 21–24, with drawings of ten such amulets.

53. It is not entirely clear whether it is fear or intoxication which leads to his incontinence.

54. For a recent summary of the abundant evidence see William

Fulco, *The Canaanite God Reśep* (New Haven: American Oriental Society, 1976).

55. This problematic epithet *(rśp ḥṣ)* is discussed in ibid., pp. 49-51.

56. UT [51].VIII.1-37, following the translation of Pope in the article "Mot," *IDBS*.

57. Such persons are condemned in various ANE law codes (e.g., MAL, A47, *ANET,* p. 184).

58. There are several ancient collections of such texts, the best known entitled Maqlu and Shurpu. The former consists of about a hundred incantations, meant to be recited over several days: see Tzvi Abusch, "Mesopotamian Anti-Witchcraft Literature, Part I: The Nature of Maqlu," *JNES* 33 (1974): 251-62.

59. Extracted from Lambert, "An Incantation of the Maqlu Type," *AfO* 18 (1958): 288-97.

60. For the idea that the underworld is an integration of all tombs see R. H. Charles, *Eschatology* (New York: Schocken Books, 1963; first published in 1899 as *The Doctrine of a Future Life in Israel, in Judaism, and in Christianity),* pp. 31-33. In any case, the descriptions of the underworld seem to be patterned after observation of rock-hewn tombs: it is "below," dark, dusty or slimy, silent, a "place of no return," and contains maggots (Isa. 14:11).

61. For a brief discussion of this term see Kilmer, "Mesopotamian Concept of Overpopulation," pp. 162-65.

62. E.g., the Gnostics, who believed that humans are bearers of a spark of divine light which has at human birth entered the realm of matter, sin, and darkness. See H. Leisegang, *Die Gnosis* (Leipzig: A. Kröner, 1924), pp. 361-62.

63. S. G. F. Brandon, *The Judgment of the Dead* (New York: Charles Scribner's Sons, 1967), p. 50.

64. For various explanations of the origin of the idea of life after death see John Hick, *Death and Eternal Life* (New York: Harper & Row, Publishers, 1976), chap. 3.

65. Quoted in *CAD,* E, p. 399.

66. Gilgamesh Epic, XII.83-85; *ANET,* p. 98; contrast *CAD,* Z, p. 59.

67. Similarly, when the "ghost" of Samuel is summoned from the

underworld by the witch at Endor, she remarks that she sees a "god" arising from the earth (1 Sam. 28:13).

68. Thompson, *Devils and Evil Spirits,* 2, Tablet Y; also quoted in 1:xxviii–xxix.

69. Just as in Israel Saul sought the opinion of the deceased prophet Samuel concerning the outcome of an impending battle (1 Sam. 28:5–7, 15–19).

70. Quoted with slight adaptation from *CAD,* E, p. 397.

71. See esp. Harry Hoffner, Jr., "Second Millennium Antecedents of the Hebrew '*ÔB,*" *JBL* 86 (1967): 385–401; and (briefly) "Familiar Spirit" in *IDBS.*

72. Hittite *a-a-bi,* Assyrian *abu,* Hebrew '*ôb* (translated "a medium" or "a spirit" in 1 Sam. 28:3, 7, 8, in KJV). Note how, above, the "ghost" of Enkidu ascends through "a hole in the earth."

73. *The Odyssey,* trans. Samuel Butler, rev. Malcolm Willcock (New York: Washington Square Press, 1964), pp. 112–15.

74. *ANET,* p. 97.

75. See above, and *CAD,* E, p. 398b; for such belief among the Sumerians see Kramer, *The Sumerians* (Chicago: University of Chicago Press, 1963), p. 134.

76. Kramer, *The Sumerians;* and esp. Lloyd Bailey, "Gehenna," in *IDBS.*

77. Kramer, *The Sumerians,* pp. 133–34, 147, for such belief among the Sumerians. Compare the Greek idea of the ferryman Charon who steers the deceased to the underworld.

78. *ANET,* p. 26.

79. Ibid., p. 110.

80. For the account of how he came to be the consort of the underworld goddess see "Nergal and Ereshkigal," *ANET,* pp. 103–4; for discussion, Jacobsen, *Treasures,* pp. 229–30. The story explains, most likely, the period of invisibility of the planet Mars (he is visiting the realm of his wife, beneath), and is related to biblical stories of a heavenly figure (the Satan) who is removed from his heavenly sphere.

81. Kramer, *The Sumerians,* pp. 131–32, 135.

82. For Sumerian belief, ibid., p. 132.

83. In general see C. J. Bleeker, "Some Remarks on the Religious Significance of Light, *ANESJ* 5 (1973): 23–34.

84. As quoted in Bayliss, "Cult of Dead Kin."

85. Quoted in *CAD,* E, p. 398.

86. AOAT, XI. For the idea that a cult city gives its name to the realm of the underworld deity beneath (e.g., Kutu and the Judeo-Christian Gehenna) see Bailey, "Gehenna," in *IDBS.*

## CHAPTER 3. DEATH IN THE LITERATURE OF
## THE OLD TESTAMENT

1. The classic in the field is R. H. Charles, *The Doctrine of a Future Life in Israel, in Judaism, and in Christianity* (1899; 2d ed., London: A. and C. Black, 1913). See below, note 14. It was republished in 1963 under the title *Eschatology* (New York: Schocken Books), with a preface (30 pp.) by G. W. Buchanan, who reviews subsequent thought about eschatology in general but has little to say about Charles's assumptions and conclusions about life after death, some of which are doubtful to erroneous. A more reliable place to begin would be Walther Eichrodt, *Theology of the Old Testament,* 2 vols. (Philadelphia: Westminster Press, 1961–67), vol. 1, chaps. 16, 19, 24.

2. Brief treatment of this much rarer approach may be found in Walter Brueggemann, "Death, Theology of," in *IDBS;* Lloyd Bailey, "Death as a Theological Problem in the Old Testament," *Pastoral Psychology* 22 (November 1971): 20–32.

3. A classic attempt to recover pre-Yahwistic survivals in Israelite religion is Adolphe Lods, *Israel* (London: Routledge and Kegan Paul, 1932), pp. 113–18, 218–30. More recently, see H. C. Brichto, "Kin, Cult, Land and Afterlife—A Biblical Complex," *HUCA* 44 (1973): 1–54.

4. For studies of some of the tensions within the postexilic community see Paul Hanson, *The Dawn of Apocalyptic* (Philadelphia: Fortress Press, 1975); Morton Smith, *Palestinian Parties and Policies that Shaped the Old Testament* (New York: Columbia University Press, 1971).

5. This issue will be discussed briefly below when we study the transition toward apocalyptic eschatology.

6. E. F. Sutcliffe, *The Old Testament and the Future Life,* 2d ed. (Westminster, Md.: Newman Bookshop, 1947), pp. 191–92. Emphases mine.

7. For particulars see James Barr, *The Bible in the Modern World* (New York: Harper & Row, publishers, 1973).

8. Thus Brueggemann, "Death, Theology of," remarks, "It is a natural part of life and is not particularly feared." See also Bailey, "Death as a Theological Problem."

9. Thus E. Jacob speaks of "an attenuation of the horror inspired by death" in "Death," *IDB*, sec. 4; Bruce Vawter remarks, "Israel's view on death was to see it as an unmitigated misfortune," in "Post-exilic Prayer and Hope," *CBQ* 37 (1975): 470; H. W. Wolff, *Anthropology of the Old Testament* (Philadelphia: Fortress Press, 1973), p. 102: "In general the Old Testament sees death in all its hideousness."

10. This is the usual position among scholars, and will be taken by the author (below).

11. Mitchell Dahood, *Psalms, AB* 16-17A, and esp. 17A, pp. xli–lii. For evaluation of his approach see esp. Vawter, "Intimations of Immortality and the Old Testament," *JBL* 91 (1972): 158–71; more generally, see reviews in *USQR* 23 (1968): 389–90 (by Terrien); *JBL* 85 (1966): 455–66, and esp. pp. 462–63 (by Pope); *Perspective* 12 (1971): 105–20 (by Campbell).

12. Milton Gatch, *Death* (New York: Seabury Press, 1969), p. 35. Generally, the volume is a helpful, clearly written introduction, which is subtitled, "Meaning and Mortality in Christian Thought and Contemporary Culture."

13. A parade example is Helmut Thielicke, *Death and Life* (Philadelphia: Fortress Press, 1970), who has a section entitled "*The* Biblical View" (pp. 32–34; emphasis mine). He remarks that "biblical man experienced death as *the* enemy" (p. 33; emphasis his), a "terrifying" threat to the "I." As far as I can tell, the threat is not perceived in that fashion anywhere in the Scriptures, and least of all in the OT.

14. R. H. Charles, *Eschatology.* See esp. pp. 9, 15, 17, 35–36, 44. See also Sutcliffe's remarks (sec. 4 above).

15. Briefly, see Norman Gottwald, "Biblical Theology or Biblical Sociology?" *Radical Religion* 2, nos. 2–3 (1975): 53; Yehezkel Kaufmann, *The Religion of Israel* (Chicago: University of Chicago Press, 1960), pp. 311–17, who describes some of the differences as "astonishing"; Bailey, "Mortality and the Fear of Death," in *Death and Ministry*, ed. J. D. Bane et al. (New York: Seabury Press, 1975), pp. 252–60.

16. Lods, *Israel;* Brichto, "Kin, Cult, Land and Afterlife."

17. As seemingly does Jacob, "Immortality," in *IDB*, p. 689a. Dahood (*AB* 16–17A) speaks of "resurrection and immortality" with little differentiation.

18. For the contrast, drawn in the strongest of terms, see Oscar Cullmann, "Immortality of the Soul or Resurrection of the Dead," in *Immortality and Resurrection,* ed. Krister Stendahl (New York: Macmillan Co., paperback, 1965), pp. 9–53. For a brief response to his position see below, chap. 6.

19. For a general discussion of the term in its ANE context see R. Norris, "Immortality," in *IDBS*.

20. This seems to be the absolute distinction intended by the well-known hymn which begins, "Immortal, invisible, God only wise."

21. Gilgamesh Epic, X.iii.1–5, OB (*ANET,* p. 90).

22. For example, when the creator-god Marduk slays the ancestress of the gods, Tiamat (Enuma Elish IV.93–104, *ANET,* p. 67), or her henchman, Kingu (VI.31–33, *ANET,* p. 68). Similarly, the Greeks had traditions about the graves of such deities as Zeus and Dionysus.

23. Gilgamesh Epic XI.190–98, *ANET,* p. 95. Only by a special granting of immortality to Utnapishtim can the god Enlil keep his oath to destroy all mortals.

24. Aqhat A.vi.26–27 (*ANET,* p. 151). The goddess makes promises to Aqhat in compensation for his bow, which she covets. "Ask for life and I'll give it to thee, for deathlessness *(bl-mt),* and I'll bestow't on thee." But Aqhat doubts that even a deity can accomplish such a feat, and he rejects her offer.

25. Enoch (Gen. 5:24) and Elijah (2 Kings 2:1–12). However, it is not beyond the realm of possibility that the texts are using formalized idioms originally at home in foreign belief-systems, which have now come to mean little more than "X died." The verb *lāqaḥ,* "to take" (Gen. 5:24) can have such a meaning (1 Kings 19:4).

26. For a brief introduction to the range of opinion see G. Nickelsburg, "Future Life in Intertestamental Literature," in *IDBS*.

27. Werner Jaeger, "The Greek Ideas of Immortality," in *Immortality and Resurrection,* ed. Stendahl, pp. 97–114.

28. For an excellent and clearly written treatment of 1 Corin-

thians 15 against this background see Leander Keck, "New Testament Views of Death," in *Perspectives on Death*, ed. Liston Mills (Nashville: Abingdon Press, 1966), pp. 61–80.

29. Norris, "Immortality," sec. 4.

30. The clearest statement of this definition may be found in Brichto's article ("Kin, Cult, Land and Afterlife"), which will be referred to several times below. For his specific use of the term to characterize the OT view of the dead see p. 3. It must be recognized that this view is quite distinct from the previous one, no. (3), which perceives that a constituent part of human beings (a "soul") is unaffected by death and usually returns to a divine realm of happiness. Here, however, no detachable part survives, but rather the "person" in its weakest possible state (see below, sec. E, on anthropology). Furthermore, it is a negative severance from the divine realm.

31. See below; for the Assyro-Babylonian descendant who serves as *paqīdu* ("[tomb] attendant") see chap. 2. Note especially the subtitle of Stanley Frost's article, "The Memorial of the Childless Man: A Study in Hebrew Thought on Immortality," *Interpretation* 26 (1972): 437–50.

32. Gilgamesh Epic III.iv.13–14, *ANET*, p. 79. See Hope Wolff, "Gilgamesh, Enkidu, and the Heroic Life," *JAOS* 89 (1969): 392–98.

33. Cited in Gatch, *Death*, p. 25. He describes such views as "civic immortality" (p. 20).

34. See Nicolas Tromp, *Primitive Conceptions of Death and the Netherworld in the Old Testament* (Rome: Pantifical Biblical Institute, 1969), pp. 160, 166.

35. For the debate about the appropriateness of this term to describe the religion of early Israel see H. Ringgren, "Monotheism," *IDBS*. For the history of the covenant idea see G. Mendenhall, "Covenant," *IDB*.

36. For the position that such "death" and "resurrection" language is not to be taken literally but is a poetic parallel to the clause which follows see below.

37. There was, however, need to acknowledge Yahweh's sovereignty, his freedom, his mysteriousness. See Paul Volz, *Das Dämonische in Jahwe* (Tübingen: J. C. B. Mohr, 1924).

38. William Culican, "Phoenician Demons," *JNES* 35 (1976): 22 (and fig. 1g).

39. For brief discussion see Theodor H. Gaster, "Demon, Demonology," *IDB*, p. 818.

40. For brief discussion see ibid.

41. MT has *sh<sup>e</sup>ʿārîm* (lit. "gates," as in RSV). The context is better fitted by *ś<sup>e</sup>ʿîrîm* ("satyrs"). The two forms would have been indistinguishable prior to the Masoretic interpretation (addition of vowels, accents, etc.) of the sixth to eighth centuries A.D.

42. See chap. 2, n. 54. For Deber see "Demon, Demonology," *IDB*, I, p. 820.

43. Patrick Miller, *The Divine Warrior in Early Israel* (Cambridge: Harvard University Press, 1973), pp. 118–19.

44. William Fulco, *The Canaanite God Rešep*, pp. 57–58, 61.

45. See Gaster, *"Demon, Demonology," IDB*, I, p. 818b (sec. 4a), who correctly observes, "Demons often survive as figures of speech (e.g., 'gremlins') long after they have ceased to be figures of belief."

46. See chap. 2 for the epithet "Resheph of the arrow."

47. For brief discussion see Fulco, *Rešep*, p. 58, and esp. n. 310, suggesting how this text has influenced the way that many of the ancient versions have translated other passages.

48. Briefly, see E. A. Speiser, *"Pālil* and Congeners: a Sampling of Apotropaic Symbols," *Studies in Honor of Benno Landsberger*, Assyriological Studies 16 (Chicago: University of Chicago Press, 1965), pp. 389–93.

49. See Jacob Milgrom, "The Book of Leviticus," *IOVCB*, pp. 70b, 73a; "Leviticus," *IDBS*, p. 543a. For contamination resulting from contact with the dead see Emanuel Feldman, *Biblical and Post-Biblical Defilement and Mourning: Law as Theology* (New York: Yeshiva University Press, 1977).

50. F. van der Meer, *Augustine the Bishop* (London: Sheed & Ward, 1961), chap. 18, for evidence of such belief at that late period.

51. For this oracular implement see I. Mendelsohn, "Urim and Thummim," *IDB*.

52. Hebrew *'ob*, mistranslated as "spirit" in the KJV. For the ANE background materials see above, chap. 2, n. 71.

53. In Akkadian texts as well, the "spirits" of the dead are sometimes called "gods," as are the demons of the underworld. For the former see Alexander Heidel, *The Gilgamesh Epic and Old Testament Parallels* (Chicago: University of Chicago Press, Phoenix Books, 1963), pp. 153, 196. For the latter, various incantations in R. Campbell Thomson, *Devils and Evil Spirits of Babylonia,* 2 vols. (London: Luzac & Co., 1904–5); e.g., "[Be exorcised,]...evil Demon [alu], evil Ghost [eṭemmu: GIDIM], evil God [ilu: DINGIR],..." (1:3). Heidel, however, wants to render the term in 1 Sam. as "(man of) God" (*Gilgamesh Epic,* p. 197), in plain disagreement to the meaning of the text.

54. Brichto, "Kin, Cult, Land and Afterlife," p. 8. At p. 28 he argues that the use of the term *god* for the deceased Samuel indicates not merely efficaciousness but a sanction for such practice (if done within the confines of an Israelite family!).

55. For recent investigation and evaluation of the claims of modern psychics, mediums, and so forth, see various issues of *The Humanist* for 1966–67.

56. Hans Walter Wolff, *Anthropology of the Old Testament,* trans. Margaret Kohl (Philadelphia: Fortress Press, 1974), p. 104.

57. So Brichto, "Kin, Cult, Land and Afterlife." See esp. pp. 8, 28.

58. For recent discussion of Israel's similarities and differences with neighbors see esp. Gottwald, "Biblical Theology or Biblical Sociology?" pp. 42–57. For explicit statement that Israel's reticence concerning rites for the dead is related to an awareness of the dangers of the religious environment see esp. Eichrodt, *Theology of the Old Testament,* 2:216–17. And it could be argued that Brichto's position (above) is a modification of this perspective. For Israel's rejection of "pagan" modes of divination see Kaufmann, *Religion of Israel,* pp. 87–93.

59. Vawter, "Intimations of Immortality," p. 170. Brichto's position (see above) is obviously in tension with this (see his remarks in "Kin, Cult, Land and Afterlife," pp. 7–8). However, Brichto himself uses the term *superstition* on p. 49 to refer to necromancy!

60. See Job 14:21 for the belief that while the dead have some vague sense of their own situation, they know nothing of the world above.

61. For this evaluation of the Bible's response to magic, Kaufmann, *Religion of Israel,* p. 79.

62. For a survey see Jacob, "Mourning," *IDB.*

63. For such belief among modern Semites see Julian Morgenstern, *Rites of Birth, Marriage, Death and Kindred Occasions among the Semites* (Cincinnati: HUC Press, 1966), pp. 136–45 (with discussion of "cult of the dead in ancient Israel" at pp. 145–49). For discussion of OT see Miriam Seligson, *The Meaning of* נפש מת *in the OT,* Studia Orientalia 16:2 (Helsinki: Societas Orientalis Fennica, 1951).

64. In agreement with Kaufmann, *Religion of Israel,* pp. 311–16, as opposed to Brichto, "Kin, Cult, Land and Afterlife." The latter proposes that biblical opposition to rites for the dead is largely limited to "connection with foreign families and *their* ancestor cults" (p. 28). "The Israelite conception of immortality...is of a piece with the cloth of pagan conceptions, conceptions inseparable from divine ancestors to whom worship is paid and sacrifices offered" (p. 49). Thus the traditional commandment "Honor your father and mother" (Exod. 20:12) means, to him, providing appropriate "funerary or memorial rites" at their tomb and preserving the patrimonial estate to which the happiness of the deceased is tied (pp. 30–31)! Part of the uniqueness of the biblical conception, he suggests, is that unlike that of neighboring peoples for whom there was no connection between this-worldly morality and otherworldly fate, it "made one's condition in the afterlife contingent not only upon his own obedience" but upon that of his descendants (p. 50). While Brichto's analysis is often provocative, it relies heavily upon an assumed pattern of common thought in the ANE, as articulated for the ancient Indo-Europeans by Fustel de Coulanges in 1864. This model is then "read into" the biblical text, or so it seems to me, despite disclaimers by the author. The interpretation of Exod. 20:12 given above is a possible example.

65. When tithes of grain were brought to the altar, symbolizing Yahweh's rightful ownership, one had to attest that none of it had been offered at the tomb of the dead (Deut. 26:12–14). This has led some scholars to suggest that other types of food, since not proscribed, were allowable. E.g., Kaufmann (*Religion of Israel,* pp. 313–14) suggests that such food would have been considered as no

more than an appropriate "gift" rather than a sacrifice. See also Brichto, "Kin, Cult, Land and Afterlife," p. 29. For an extended treatment of banquets for the dead in ancient Israel (and Semites in general) see Marvin Pope, *Song of Songs, AB* 7C.

66. For very brief discussion see Gottwald, "Biblical Theology or Biblical Sociology," p. 53.

67. For general discussion of this type of literature see J. Priest, "Etiology," *IDBS*. It usually gives an entertaining folk explanation of some present custom or edifice by tracing its origin back to a formative event in the past. For example, a child might ask, "Why does the bear have a short tail, in contrast to most other animals?" An American Indian etiological account tells us that the bear used an originally long tail as a fishing line but broke it off when it became encased in the ice. Or again, "How did the city of Bethel (meaning 'Temple of God') get its name?" An etiological account in Genesis 28 tells us that Jacob slept on a stone (apparently in an open field) and had a dream in which God appeared to him, whereupon he erected an altar to God. Archaeologically, however, the city is much older than the usual dates for the patriarchal age (early second millennium B.C.), and thus we see that such an account is not "historical" in the modern sense of that term.

68. This possibility is developed at some length by Eduard Nielsen, "Creation and the Fall of Man," *HUCA* 43 (1972): 1–22. For introductory background on the composite nature of the accounts in Genesis–Deuteronomy see the following *IDBS* articles: "Yahwist"; "Elohist"; "Priestly Writers"; "Source Criticism."

69. For details see Nielsen, "Creation and the Fall of Man," pp. 15–17.

70. Since the word is used with the definite article in the account in Genesis 2–3, and since it is not used in the plural or to denote individuals otherwise in the OT, it has been plausibly argued that the ancient Israelite hearers would not have understood the story to refer to a biological individual but rather to a typological "human" who is treated *as if* an individual. See Alison Grant, "'*Adam* and '*ish:* Man in the OT," *Australian Biblical Review* 25 (October 1977): 2–11. In later biblical material, however, the article is dropped (e.g., Gen. 5:1) and the word is apparently treated like a proper name (Adam).

71. The word can also mean, and is more usually translated, "dust." The former more closely fits the imagery here.

72. Thus the humans are not intentionally set apart by this procedure, contrary to the interpretation of most scholars, e.g., Hans Walter Wolff (*Anthropology,* p. 94): "But the beasts do not receive the divine breath of life." Not only is this alleged distinction based upon a silence in the text, but it seems to assume that in the biblical understanding the other creatures generated life spontaneously—which could be seen as an innate superiority over humans! For further discussion of the anthropological views of Genesis 1–3, see below.

73. Some readers may recall that the KJV (and other versions) describes "the man" as a "living soul" (Gen. 2:7) but the other animals as "moving creatures" (1:20) or as "living creatures" (1:24). However, the same Hebrew word is used in both places *(nephesh hayyah),* and thus the KJV, under the influence of later anthropological views, introduces a distinction which the Genesis writer never intended.

74. For support for this position see, e.g., Umberto Cassuto, *A Commentary on the Book of Genesis* (Jerusalem: Magnes Press, 1961), 1. Such a continuous reading apparently leads Otto Kaiser and Edward Lohse to conclude that although creation included mortality, it is sin which makes it terrifying: *Tod und Leben* (Stuttgart: W. Kohlhammer, 1977), pp. 16–17.

75. Contrast the opinion of *The New Catholic Encyclopedia,* s.v. "Death," where death in general is said to have "flowed from God's wrath and was provoked by primeval as well as personal sins." However, the texts cited in support (Prov. 2:18; 7:27; 21:16; 22:23; Isa. 5:14) will not bear this interpretation.

76. See *Encyclopaedia Judaica,* s.v. "Death."

77. The latter passage goes well beyond Genesis not only in identifying the serpent as a malign being but also with the recently developed idea of a "devil."

78. Perhaps it would be more accurate from a modern scholarly point of view to describe it as historicized myth, that is, primeval stories that have been placed in a "chronological" sequence and made to serve as a preface to Israel's "story."

79. For an example see below, sec. F.

80. For the idea that Sheol may once have been a proper name

for the underworld deity (cf. the Greek god Hades who gave his name to his realm) see Tromp, *Primitive Conceptions of Death,* p. 22. For illustrations of how deities or demons of the neighbors have been demythologized (de-divinized) and reduced to common nouns see the discussion of demons above (sec. B).

81. For use of the Hebrew *'ereṣ* in this sense see Tromp, *Primitive Conceptions of Death,* pp. 23–46.

82. For this designation see ibid., pp. 66–71.

83. Text quoted in *VT* 17 (1967): 226ff. For a general discussion of the ANE understanding of "death" in this sense see Heidel, *Gilgamesh Epic,* pp. 207–10.

84. For full discussion see Rudolph Bultmann, *Life and Death* (London: Adam Charles Black, 1965).

85. A "weakening" that seemed to continue even in the tomb (see below).

86. Tromp, *Primitive Conceptions of Death,* pp. 114ff., suggests several passages in which he thinks that "death" is depicted as a powerful force. See also Christoph Barth, *Die Errettung von Tode in die individuellen Klage- und Dankliedern des alten Testaments* (Zollikon: Evangelischer Verlag, 1947), who describes death as a "realm" of opposition to the living.

87. For brief mention of this deity see chap. 2 above; Pope, "Mot," *IDBS.*

88. For the same verb *(yāṣar)* used of a potter see Jer. 18.

89. For the Atrahasis account see chap. 2.

90. In general see J. Sasson, "Wordplay in the OT," *IDBS.*

91. For the same distinction see chap. 2.

92. In general see the discussion in Hans Walter Wolff, *Anthropology,* chaps. 2, 4; Eichrodt, *Theology of the Old Testament,* vol. 2, chap. 16.

93. For the related idea that God "breathed into" all animals, not merely man, resulting in "life" *(nephesh),* see above.

94. The usual etymology, as proposed by Hans Walter Wolff, *Anthropology,* pp. 11–14. It has, however, been challenged (e.g., by Seligson).

95. For this particular developmental equation see Georg Fohrer, *History of Israelite Religion,* trans. David E. Green (Nashville: Abingdon Press, 1972), p. 215.

96. Charles, *Eschatology,* pp. 39–47.

97. Hans Walter Woff, *Anthropology,* p. 33.

98. E.g., Charles, *Eschatology,* p. 39; cf. p. 42.

99. E.g., Seligson, *Meaning.*

100. The verb is *yāṣa'.*

101. *Yāṣa'.*

102. Most English translations use the word *spirit* here, a nebulous term which could easily result in later anthropological views being projected into the text.

103. An alternative translation could be, "No one knows..."

104. We may see here a literary vestige of the Canaanite perspective: the life-force is seized by the underworld god Mot (lit. "Death").

105. As translated in Heidel, *Gilgamesh Epic,* p. 156, citing Rawlinson, V, Pl. 6, col. vi (pp. 70-76). For many other examples see chap. 2.

106. For burial practices in the ANE see Heidel, *Gilgamesh Epic,* pp. 150-70 (Assyro-Babylonion); E. Meyers, "Tomb," *IDBS* (Palestinian); J. Callaway, "Burials in Ancient Palestine," *BA* 26 (1963): 74-91.

107. Occasionally an Akkadian text does speak of the *nepishtu* (cognate to the Hebrew *nephesh*) descending to the underworld, e.g., in Shalmaneser III's account of the slaughter at the battle of Qarqar (*ANET,* p. 279).

108. For this idea as well as Sheol as an ancient deity see above, n. 80.

109. Wolfram Herrmann, "Human Mortality as a Problem in Ancient Israel," in *Religious Encounters with Death,* ed. F. Reynolds and E. Waugh (University Park: Pennsylvania State University Press, 1977), pp. 161-69.

110. See esp. Hildegard Lewy, "Points of Comparison between Zoroastrianism and the Moon-cult of Harran," in *A Locust's Leg,* (London: Percy Lund, Humphries & Co., 1962), pp. 139-61.

111. In general see M. Greenberg, "Bloodguilt," *IDB.*

112. Since it contained the life-force, which belonged intrinsically to God. See D. J. McCarthy, "Blood," *IDBS.*

113. See M. Greenberg, "Crimes and Punishments," sec. D1, *IDB.*

114. For general discussion, including evidence that others could provide such service for the dead, see Miranda Bayliss, "The Cult of Dead Kin in Assyria and Babylonia," *Iraq* 35 (1973): 115-25. In pa-

triarchal societies, as most of those in the ANE were, it is not surprising that sons would be assigned this responsibility. For a study of the effects of patriarchal social structure upon biblical literature see Phyllis Trible, "Depatriarchalizing in Biblical Interpretation," *JAAR* 41 (1973): 30–48.

115. See, however, Brichto's position (above).

116. For a brief but convenient summary see V. Kooy, "Firstborn," *IDB*.

117. While this is well attested in Mesopotamia (see above, chap. 2), it is scarcely so in the OT. See C. F. D. Moule, "Adoption," *IDB*.

118. Perhaps the most famous case in the Bible is that of Hagar, who serves to overcome the barrenness of Sarah (Gen. 16:1–4).

119. In general see O. J. Baab, "Marriage," sec. 1g, *IDB*. For a study of the problem posed when this institution became less acceptable see Frost, "Memorial to the Childless Man."

120. "The threat is never the simple possibility of death through old age." Walther Zimmerli, *The Old Testament and the World* (Atlanta: John Knox Press, 1976), p. 117.

121. For a brief introduction to this type of theological problem see J. Crenshaw, "Theodicy," *IDBS*.

122. The rabbis surmised that Sheol was created on the second day, since the expression "it was good" is missing in its description. While this may indicate they perceived Sheol to be other than "good," it nonetheless was a divinely ordained part of the structure of things.

123. In contrast to George Coats, "Death and Dying in Old Testament Tradition," *Lexington Theological Quarterly* 11 (1976): 9–14. He cites in particular Psalm 90: "You have set our iniquities before you.... Truly all our days have passed away in your wrath; we have ended our years like a sigh" (vv. 8–9). But to remark that life is characterized by difficulty, perceived as divine wrath, is not to state that every death, indeed death itself, is a punishment. To be sure, later generations, in the New Testament and Rabbinic periods, would make such a connection. A connection between mortality and sin is also asserted in the article "Death (in the Bible)," *New Catholic Encyclopedia* (1967 ed.).

124. See above, n. 68, on the possibility of two etiologies which

have been combined in the Yahwist's account. Hans Walter Wolff (*Anthropology,* pp. 115–16) seems to recognize such a dual interpretation.

125. For an allusion to this reality in Mesopotamian literature see "Inanna's Descent" (*ANET,* p. 55) or "Ishtar's Descent" (pp. 107–8), where the dead arrive naked at the underworld.

126. For the categories "death-accepting," "death-denying," and "death-defying" to describe various societies' response to death see Robert J. Fulton and Robert Bendiksen, eds., *Death and Identity,* rev. ed. (Bowie, Md.: Charles Press Publishers, 1976), pp. 42ff. For similar but more detailed attempts to categorize attitudes see Edwin Shneidman, "The Enemy," *Psychology Today,* August 1970, pp. 37–41, 62–66.

127. This is stressed at length in Leviticus 17–26, often called "The Holiness Code."

128. "Life" as relatedness and "death" as relationlessness is stressed by Eberhard Jüngel, *Death: The Riddle and the Mystery* (Philadelphia: Westminster Press, 1974).

129. So Eichrodt, *Theology of the Old Testament,* 2:522–29; Terrien, *The Elusive Presence* (San Francisco: Harper & Row, Publishers, 1978), pp. 366–71 (discussing Psalm 73).

130. See esp. Norbert Lohfink, *The Christian Meaning of the Old Testament* (Milwaukee: Bruce Publishing Co., 1969), chap. 8.

131. The verb used in all these citations is *laqaḥ;* so also in Gen. 5:24, where Enoch is "taken" by the Deity.

132. Eichrodt, *Theology of the Old Testament,* 2:232–36 ("Solidarity Thinking in Israel's Environment").

133. For the various articulations of the promise see Claus Westermann, "Promise to the Patriarchs," *IDBS.* For greater detail see his *Blessing: In the Bible and the Life of the Church* (Philadelphia: Fortress Press, 1978).

134. There is a long-standing problem of interpretation here: is the blessing to be exclusive (NEB) or inclusive (LXX)? Briefly, see Gerhard von Rad, *Genesis* (Philadelphia: Westminster Press, 1961), pp. 155–56. Contrast his interpretation with that of Westermann, "Promise to the Patriarchs," sec. 3e.

135. This response, attributed to Moses in Israel's early canonical

literature and probably indicative of the mood of the time, is in strong contrast to the much later Rabbinic work entitled "The Death of Moses," in which Moses refuses to obey the death-angel who is sent directly by God to summon him.

136. See esp. Frost, "Memorial to the Childless Man."

137. Brueggemann, "The Formfulness of Grief," *Interpretation* 31 (1977): 265. He goes on to compare and contrast the elements of the lament-form with the stages of the grieving process as observed by Kübler-Ross.

138. Various possible bases for this shift from petition to praise are briefly but conveniently outlined by Brueggemann, "From Hurt to Joy, From Death to Life," *Interpretation* 28 (1974): 9.

139. It seems to me that Brueggemann (in "The Formfulness of Grief") slips beyond the OT period when he remarks that "Israel's perception [was] of death as a conquered enemy" (p. 273). He apparently is speaking of biological death as perceived in Israel's laments.

140. Artur Weiser, *The Psalms* (Philadelphia: Westminster Press, 1962), pp. 596, 601, 602.

## CHAPTER 4. THE TRANSITION TOWARD APOCALYPTIC ESCHATOLOGY

1. The terms *eschatology* (lit. "the furtherest, or last things") and *apocalyptic* (lit. "uncovered, revealed") have no commonly agreed-upon definition in recent scholarly thought. They may overlap to a large degree or be set in tension at points. For a brief review see John Collins, "Apocalyptic Eschatology as the Transcendence of Death," *CBQ* 36 (1974): 21–30, and especially the literature there cited.

2. This distinction is roughly that of Paul Hanson, *The Dawn of Apocalyptic* (Philadelphia: Fortress Press, 1975). Briefly, see his article "Apocalypticism," *IDBS*.

3. For a brief review of the debate about the extent of Israel's conformity to or distinctiveness from an alleged theology common to the ANE see Norman Gottwald, "Biblical Theology or Biblical Sociology?" *Radical Religion* 2, nos. 2–3 (1975): 42–57.

4. For a study of the Jacob traditions from both perspectives see Terry Fretheim, "The Jacob Traditions," *Interpretation* 26 (1972): 419–36.

5. For a brief study of the various layers of tradition see Claus Westermann, "Promises to the Patriarchs," *IDBS*.

6. See Walther Zimmerli, *The Old Testament and the World* (Atlanta: John Knox Press, 1976), chap. 10, "The Hope of Israel and the Hope of the World."

7. How many migrations there were and their dates, as well as whether all of Israel's "ancestors" participated in them, are currently matters of scholarly debate which need not detain us here.

8. James A. Sanders, *Studies in Divine Discipline in the Old Testament and Post-Biblical Judaism* (Rochester: Colgate Rochester Divinity School, 1955).

9. Hans Walter Wolff, "The Understanding of History in the Prophets," in *Essays on Old Testament Hermeneutics,* ed. Westermann (Richmond: John Knox Press, 1963), p. 341.

10. For details, Hanson, *Dawn of Apocalyptic;* William Millar, *Isaiah 24—27 and the Origin of Apocalyptic* (Missoula: Scholars Press, 1976).

11. For a brief introduction to this figure of Canaanite mythology see Theodor H. Gaster, "Leviathan," *IDB:* see also his articles "Dragon" and "Cosmogony," *IDB.* More generally, see M. Wakeman, "Chaos," *IDBS*.

12. Briefly, see J. Jeremias, "Theophany in the OT," sec. 2, *IDBS;* for detail, Patrick Miller, *The Divine Warrior in Early Israel* (Cambridge University Press, 1973).

13. That the majority did not and remained in Babylon is clear from the fact that Babylonia remained the intellectual and religious center of Jewish life until the Middle Ages.

14. For a brief introduction see E. Rivkin, "Aaron, Aaronides," *IDBS*.

15. For discussion of the social setting of apocalypticism see Hanson, "Apocalypticism." One need not assume that this group was made up of returnees only.

16. For brief discussion see Hanson, *Dawn of Apocalyptic,* p. 323.

17. Reading the jussive mood rather than indicative, in conformity with the context, as opposed to most interpreters. See Millar, *Isaiah 24—27,* p. 53.

18. MT: "my."

19. Reading as jussive, in agreement with IQIsa[a], as opposed to the imperative of MT.

20. For this translation ("[Elysian] Fields" instead of "light") see Mitchell Dahood, *Psalms I, AB* 16, pp. 222–23.

21. Dates assigned by modern scholars range from the sixth and fifth centuries to the second century B.C.

22. The translation and strophic structure is that of Millar, *Isaiah 24–27,* pp. 40–42.

23. E.g., by Otto Kaiser, *Isaiah 13–39* (Philadelphia: Westminster Press, 1974), p. 199. However, it may form an "inclusion" with a previous line ("He will swallow on this mount") and thus be original.

24. The idea that the world is subdivided for oversight among the members of the divine council is in Israel's literature as old as Deut. 32:8–9, possibly borrowed from a Canaanite hymn:

When Elyon gave to the nations their inheritance,

When he separated the sons of men,

He fixed the bounds of the peoples according to the number of the sons of El.

(trans. mine)

25. Cf. Dan. 8:9–13, where the terms "host of heaven," "host of the stars," and "holy one(s)" seem to be used interchangeably. See Collins, "Apocalyptic Eschatology," and the literature cited on p. 32, n. 36. More usually "the saints of the Most High" is taken by modern scholars as a reference to the Jews who have remained faithful during the persecutions by Antiochus Epiphanes.

26. E.g., Collins, "Apocalyptic Eschatology," p. 34. More usually the description is taken as simile for the glorious life in the new Jerusalem.

## CHAPTER 5. THE INTERTESTAMENTAL LITERATURE

1. For the problem of defining such terms as apocalyptic eschatology, protoapocalyptic, and apocalypticism see Paul Hanson, "Apocalypticism," *IDBS,* and for more detail, idem, *The Dawn of Apocalyptic* (Philadelphia: Fortress Press, 1975).

2. As translated by Theodor H. Gaster, *The Dead Sea Scriptures* (Garden City: Doubleday & Co., Anchor Books, 1956), pp. 43–44.

3. For a general introduction see S. G. F. Brandon, *The Judgment of the Dead* (New York: Charles Scribner's Sons, 1967), chap. 7 ("Iran").

4. Contrary to much of the scholarship of previous generations

which saw Persian influence as a crucial factor in the development of Israel's thought.

5. For this suggestion see W. Brueggemann, "Death, Theology of," secs. 4–5, *IDBS.*

6. In the concluding clause the author is using "death" in a sense wider than biological cessation, and more in line with Israel's ancient Wisdom Literature.

7. For a brief introduction to the communal life-threatening actions of the Seleucids see N. Turner, "Antiochus," sec. 4, *IDB;* for detail, Solomon Zeitlin, *The Rise and Fall of the Judean State,* (Philadelphia: Jewish Publication Society, 1964), 1:59–93.

8. Brueggemann, "Death, Theology of," sec. 5c.

9. See Leander Keck, "New Testament Views of Death," in *Perspectives on Death,* ed. Liston Mills (Nashville: Abingdon Press, 1966), pp. 44–45.

10. In the Homeric literature this term is used not merely for the life-giving energy but also for the "shadows" [*eidōlon*] in the underworld, who are devoid of mental activity.

11. The older term *psuchē* is likewise used for this new entity, perhaps now best translated by the nebulous term "soul."

12. For a brief introduction to the full range of opinion see George Nickelsburg, "Future Life in Intertestamental Literature," *IDBS;* for more details see his *Resurrection, Immortality, and Eternal Life in Intertestamental Judaism,* Harvard Theological Studies 26 (Cambridge: Harvard University Press, 1972).

13. For the importance of obedience to Torah (or the will of God) even in the face of death, and its background for understanding a NT portrait of Jesus, see W. D. Davies, *Paul and Rabbinic Judaism,* 2d ed. (London: S.P.C.K., 1955), pp. 263–68.

14. The translation is that of Michael E. Stone, *The Testament of Abraham: the Greek Recensions,* Society of Biblical Literature Texts and Translations 2, Pseudepigrapha Series 2 (Missoula, Mont.: Scholars Press, 1972), p. 85.

15. For various attempts to date this work see *Studies On The Testament of Abraham,* ed. George Nickelsburg, Jr., Society of Biblical Literature, Septuagint and Cognate Studies VI (Missoula, Mont.: Scholars Press, 1976), pp. 15, 19.

16. For the debate about the relative age of the two recensions see

the various articles in ibid.

17. For an excellent though brief treatment of such developments see Gaster, "Demon" and "Satan," *IDB*.

18. Antecedents for this backward projection of Satan's activities could include the ancient conflict-myths (e.g., Yahweh vs. the dragon Leviathan at creation, and references to acts of judgment in the divine council such as Psalm 82). A parallel may be found in the Akkadian story of the sky-god Nergal (Mars) who descends and becomes master of the underworld (*ANET*², pp. 103-4, "Nergal and Ereshkigal"), which may have been formulated to explain the period of invisibility of the planet Mars.

19. For a brief survey of the evidence see Nickelsburg, *Resurrection, Immortality, and Eternal Life*, p. 166, n. 126.

20. Nickelsburg, "Future Life in Intertestamental Literature," sec. 4. He characterizes this view as "realized eschatology," a term often used for a perspective which occurs in the NT. See E. Fiorenza, "Eschatology in the New Testament," sec. 3c, *IDBS*.

21. That this does not mean the remains of the body in the tomb is clear from the context. Cf. Gen. 3:19 ("You are dust") as an evaluation of living mortals.

22. For this term as a designation both for the angelic hosts and the earthly community see the discussion of the Book of Daniel (above, chap. 4).

23. Or "wormy dead." Description of mortals as a mere "maggot" or "worm" are to be found in the OT (e.g., Isa. 41:14; Job 25:6). For "dead (one)" in the sense of a living "nobody" see, e.g., 2 Sam. 9:8.

24. The translation is from Nickelsburg, *Resurrection, Immortality, and Eternal Life*, pp. 154-55.

25. E.g., Chaim Rabin, *Qumran Studies* (Oxford: Oxford University Press, 1957), p. 73.

26. For brief treatment of the ancient idea of a council of divine beings surrounding Yahweh see D. Neiman, "Council, Heavenly," *IDBS*.

27. For this designation of the underworld, see Gaster, "Abaddon," *IDB*.

28. Or "I walk unhindered in the plain."

29. For the translation, Nickelsburg, *Resurrection, Immortality, and Eternal Life*, p. 152.

30. J. van der Ploeg, "Immortalité de l'homme d'après les textes de la Mer Morte," VT 2 (1952): 171–75; idem, "The Belief in Immortality in the Writings of Qumran," *BO* 18 (1961): 123.

31. See Frank Moore Cross, Jr., *The Ancient Library of Qumran* (Garden City: Doubleday & Co., Anchor Books, 1961), pp. 76–78, 198–206.

32. For an introduction to the literature see ibid., pp. 70–106.

33. Based upon the Damascus Document. See Geza Vermes, *Discovery in the Judean Desert* (New York: Desclee Co., 1956), pp. 110–11.

34. *Yā'ûrû.* The verb *'ûr*, especially in the OT, means "to arouse for action." Its use in a military context is clear from Judg. 5:12, "'Awake, awake, O Deborah!'... the people of the Lord marched ...against the mighty." By contrast Dan. 12:2 uses *qûṣ* (cf. *qûṣ* and *qûm* in Isa. 26:19) to describe a resurrection of the dead.

35. Or "mortal worms." See above, n. 23.

36. As translated in Nickelsburg, *Resurrection, Immortality, and Eternal Life,* p. 150.

37. Rabin, *Qumran Studies,* p. 73; Svend Holm-Nielsen, *Hodayot* (Aarhus: Universitetsforlanget, 1960), pp. 121–22; Menahem Mansoor, *The Thanksgiving Hymns* (Grand Rapids: Eerdmans, 1961), p. 147.

38. Those who question a reference to resurrection include Nickelsburg, *Resurrection, Immortality, and Eternal Life,* p. 151 (see his n. 45 for others of like opinion).

39. On the problematic text see above, chap. 4.

40. Nickelsburg, *Resurrection, Immortality, and Eternal Life,* pp. 144, 154, 167. Nickelsburg suggests that this lack of emphasis upon physical death is compatible with other "two-way" theologies, and in particular with a theology of immortality (as in Wisdom of Solomon) or of immediate assumption (Testament of Asher) (p. 167). It must be added, however, that these books do not have the developed messianism that one finds at Qumran, including the earthly rule of two messiahs in the city of Jerusalem. How disembodied (?) "souls" are to participate in such a renewed continuation of earthly existence remains unclear to me.

## CHAPTER 6. THE NEW TESTAMENT

1. See above, chap. 3, sec. E.

2. Although it has usually been assumed that Paul here speaks of

mortality, he may be using the word "death" in a wide metaphoric sense.

3. For an excellent exposition along these lines see Arthur McGill, "Death as Destruction and Nourishment," (an unpublished paper presented to the American Theological Society, April 4–5, 1975).

4. Compare Wisd. of Sol. 2:23–24; 1 QS III, 17–22.

5. Scholars are not unanimous in the opinion that this letter was written by Paul. In any case, a similar perspective is expressed in Col. 2:8, 15; Rom. 8:38.

6. See above, chap. 3, n. 70 (for *'adam* vs. *'is*); perhaps it would be appropriate to call the entire primeval history "myth in historical terms," since it has been set as a preface to the history of Israel. Paul may, like some modern readers, view it entirely as history.

7. For reference to this continuation as a problem see Leander Keck, "New Testament Views of Death," in *Perspectives on Death*, ed. Liston Mills (Nashville: Abingdon Press, 1969), p. 47.

8. On this complicated problem see W. D. Davies, *Paul and Rabbinic Judaism*, 2d ed. (London: S.P.C.K., 1955), chaps. 2–3.

9. For brief discussion of some of the departures, or at least modifications, see Keck, "New Testament Views of Death," esp. pp. 44–47.

10. There are, however, occasional exceptions, such as the discussion of the continuity of human relationships raised by the question concerning the woman with multiple husbands (Mark 12:18–27).

11. There is here a similarity to the OT Wisdom Literature, in which awareness of mortality may serve as an incentive to action (Eccles. 9:9–10) or to the acquisition of wisdom (Ps. 90:12).

12. Oscar Cullmann, "Immortality of the Soul or Resurrection of the Dead," in *Immortality and Resurrection*, ed. Krister Stendahl (New York: Macmillan Co., paperback, 1965), pp. 9–53.

13. For an introduction see Werner Jaeger, "The Greek Ideas of Immortality," in *Immortality and Resurrection*, ed. Stendahl, pp. 97–114.

14. Once the question of the status of the dead during the interim between death and resurrection is raised, the distinctiveness of the two doctrines begins to diminish. For the range of positions during the period between the Testaments see George Nickelsburg, *Resurrection, Immortality, and Eternal Life in Intertestamental Judaism*, Harvard Theological Studies 26 (Cambridge: Harvard University Press, 1972).

15. While it is generally understood that he refers to those who are imperceptive and unresponsive (the "spiritually" dead), another interpretation has been suggested: in the original (Aramaic) proverb the vocalization was not *l<sup>e</sup>miqbar* ("to bury") but *limqabber* ("to the burier"). Hence, "Leave the (biologically) dead to the burier of the dead." See I. Abrahams, *Studies in Pharisaism and the Gospels,* ed. Harry Orlinsky, Library of Biblical Studies, 2d series (reprint ed., New York: Ktav, 1967), p. 183, citing F. Perles.

16. The factors that produced this shift in emphasis have often been discussed by scholars: was it an experience of transforming power, with some antecedents in the literature at Qumran (already one stands with the angels) and in the writings of Paul (Christians as a new creation)? Or was it related to dissatisfaction with the delay of Christ's return (1 Thess. 4:13–18)? Predominant opinion seems to favor the former. For excellent discussion see Raymond Brown, *John I–XII, AB* 29, pp. CXV–CXXI.

17. For brief discussion of the similarities and differences in emphasis between Paul and the Gospel of John see Keck, "New Testament Views of Death," esp. pp. 84, 89, 90, 92–94.

18. McGill, "Death as Destruction and Nourishment."

19. Ibid.

## CHAPTER 7. CONCLUDING REFLECTIONS

1. In general see James A. Sanders, "Hermeneutics," *IDBS.* For the position that the final (canonical) shape of the tradition ought to be authoritative (as opposed to earlier perspectives which it may have incorporated), see Brevard Childs, *Biblical Theology in Crisis* (Philadelphia: Westminster Press, 1970), pt. II. He has recently presented his position as applied to part of the canon in brief and clear fashion in "The Canonical Shape of the Prophetic Literature," *Interpretation* 32 (1978): 46–55. A useful review of the book, calling for a fuller canonical perspective, is that of Sanders in *USQR* 26 (1971): 299–304.

2. This section is an expansion of the concluding part of my article "Death in Biblical Thought," *Encyclopedia of Bioethics,* 4 vols., ed. Warren T. Reich (New York: Macmillan Co., Free Press, 1978), pp. 243–46.

3. For a general discussion of the problem see James Barr, *The Bible in the Modern World* (New York: Harper & Row, Publishers, 1973).

4. To this must be added the fact that the Bible was not *primarily* preserved by succeeding generations as a textbook of moral examples. Briefly, see Sanders, "Hermeneutics," sec. 8g ("Theologizing and Moralizing"); for more detail, Leander Keck, *The Bible in the Pulpit* (Nashville: Abingdon Press, 1978), pp. 100–5 ("Farewell to Moralizing"). For a favorably reviewed study in method see Bruce Birch and Larry Rasmussen, *Bible and Ethics in the Christian Life* (Minneapolis: Augsburg Publishing House, 1976).

5. For a discussion of the relationship between Scripture and community (church) see David Kelsey, *The Uses of Scripture in Recent Theology* (Philadelphia: Fortress Press, 1975), chap. V.

6. The relationship between one's mental state on the one hand and proneness to illness or ability to recover from it on the other. For general resources see below, n. 15.

7. The relationship between body image (for example, post-mastectomy) and mental or social health. See S. E. Cleveland and S. F. Fisher, *Body Image and Personality* (Princeton: Van Nostrand, 1958).

8. For a review and popular presentation of various studies see David Dempsey, *The Way We Die* (New York: Macmillan Co., 1975), chap. 7.

9. *Durham Morning Herald,* September 11, 1978, p. 4A, carried by the Post-Times News Service.

10. For a questionnaire which differentiates various kinds of fear of death see Robert Neale, "Explorations in Death Education," *Pastoral Psychology* 22 (November 1971): 47–48, and discussion. For a different approach see J. Diggory and D. Rothman, "Values Destroyed by Death," *Journal of Abnormal and Social Psychology* 63 (1961): 205–10.

11. Ruth Abrams, "The Patient with Cancer—His Changing Pattern of Communication," *New England Journal of Medicine* 274, no. 6 (1966): 317–22.

12. John McKinney and Frank de Vyver, eds., *Aging and Social Policy* (New York: Appleton-Century-Crofts, 1966), pp. 302–29 ("The Social Meaning of Death and the Law").

13. M. I. Berman, "The Todeserwartung Syndrome," *Geriatrics* 21 (May, 1976): 187–92.

14. It is only as recently as the pioneering work of Elizabeth Kübler-Ross, *On Death and Dying* (New York: Macmillan Co., 1969), that a basic pattern was perceived.

15. For a popular presentation within the context of the hospital chaplaincy see the following articles by Robert Reeves, Jr.: "The Total Response," *JRH* 4, no. 3 (April 1965): 243–52; "Total Health for the Total Man," *JRH* 1, no. 4 (1966): 29–38; "What Makes the Critter Tick?" *Pastoral Psychology* (May 1963): 16–21. For a different level of presentation by a psychiatrist see Lawrence LeShan, "Mobilizing the Life Force," in *Psychosomatic Aspects of Neoplastic Disease*, ed. D. Kissen and Lawrence LeShan (New York: Lippincott, 1964).

16. Lawrence LeShan and Eda LeShan, "Psychotherapy and the Patient with a Limited Life Span," *Psychiatry Journal for the Study of Interpersonal Processes* 24, no. 4 (November 1961); also printed in *Death: Interpretations*, ed. Hendrik Ruitenbeek (New York: Delta Books, 1969), pp. 106–15.

17. An illustrative case of the deadly conspiracy of silence is told by a social worker concerning her visit with a dying patient: "I knew he wanted to talk to me, but I always turned it into something light... a little joke, or some evasive reassurance which had to fail. The patient knew, and I knew, but as the patient felt my anxiety, he kept to himself what he wanted to share with another human being... and so he died and did not bother me." Related by Elizabeth Kübler-Ross, "Dying as a Psychological Event," *The Experience of Dying*, ed. Norbert Greinacher and Alois Müller, Concilium 94 (New York: Seabury Press), p. 50.

18. For a brief introduction to the idea see Roberta Paige and Jane Looney, "Hospice Care for the Adult," *American Journal of Nursing*, November 1977, pp. 1812–15. For excellent case studies see Robert Neale, "Between the Nipple and the Everlasting Arms," *USQR* 27 (1972): 81–90.

19. For the problem of translating the sixth commandment (Exod. 20:13, "kill" [RSV] vs. "murder" [NEB]) see J. J. Stamm and M. E. Andrew, *The Ten Commandments in Recent Research* (Naperville, Ill.: Alec Allenson, 1967), pp. 98–99.

20. For the social context of this blessing (underpopulation, as opposed to overpopulation in Mesopotamia) see the following articles in sequence: Anne Draffkorn Kilmer, "The Mesopotamian Concept of Overpopulation and Its Solution as Reflected in the Mythology," *Orientalia* 41 (1972): 160–77; Tikva Frymer-Kensky, "The Atrahasis Epic and Its Significance for our Understanding of Genesis 1–9," *BA* 40 (1977): 147–55. For the historical setting of this blessing see Carol Meyers, "The Roots of Restriction: Women in Early Israel," *BA* 41 (September 1978): 91–103.

21. See *EJ,* s.v. "Autopsies and Dissection."

22. This section is an expansion of the introduction to my article "Mortality and the Fear of Death," in *Death and Ministry,* ed. J. D. Bane et al. (New York: Seabury Press, 1975), pp. 252–60.

23. For summaries see David Martin and Lawrence Wrightsman, "Religion and the Fears about Death: A Critical Review of Research," *Religious Education* 59 (1964): 174–76; David Lester, "Religious Behaviors and Attitudes Toward Death," in *Death and Presence,* ed. A. Godin (Brussels: Lumen Vitae, 1972), pp. 107–24.

24. Herman Feifel, "Attitudes toward Death in Some Normal and Mentally Ill Populations," in *The Meaning of Death,* ed. idem (New York: McGraw-Hill, paperback, 1965), p. 121.

25. Irving Alexander and Arthur Adlerstein, "Studies in the Psychology of Death," in *Perspectives in Personality Research,* ed. Henry David and J. C. Brengelmann (New York: Springer, 1960), pp. 65–92.

26. Alexander and Adlerstein, "Death and Religion," in *The Meaning of Death,* ed. Feifel, pp. 271–83.

27. See above, n. 22.

28. For the distinctions see R. S. Lazarus, *Psychological Stress and the Coping Process* (New York: McGraw-Hill Book Co., 1966); E. E. Levitt, *The Psychology of Anxiety* (London: Staples Press, 1968); C. D. Spielberger, ed., *Anxiety and Behavior* (New York: Academic Press, 1966).

29. See Neale, "Explorations in Death Education," *Pastoral Psychology* 22 (November 1971): 47–56.

30. See Klas Magni, "The Fear of Death," in *Death and Presence,* ed. Godin, pp. 125–38, esp. pp. 132–36.

31. Alexander and Adlerstein, "Death and Religion," p. 277.

32. As an illustration of the latter see Arnold Toynbee's descrip-

tion of his great-uncle in "Changing Attitudes toward Death in the Modern Western World," in *Man's Concern with Death*, ed. idem (New York: McGraw-Hill Book Co., 1968), pp. 93–94, 130.

33. For a recent poll of ten European countries showing that whereas 60 to 96 percent of the population believed in the existence of God, only 35 to 57 percent believed in life after death see Pierre Delooz, "Who Believes in the Hereafter?" in *Death and Presence*, ed. Godin, pp. 17–38. Surveys taken over a twenty-year period show that the percentage in the latter category is falling. For the assertion that there is a connection between such failing belief and increasing anxiety about death see Toynbee, "Changing Attitudes toward Death," p. 130.

34. The remainder of this section is based partly upon my article "Death as a Theological Problem in the Old Testament," *Pastoral Psychology* 22 (November 1971): 30–31. See also above, chap. 1.

35. For the problematic position that the Bible is responsible for the alienation of humans from the realm of nature (it becomes an "object" to be studied and used, rather than a "subject" to be revered) and thus ultimately for the contemporary ecological crisis see Lynn White, Jr., "The Historical Roots of Our Ecological Crisis," *Science* 155 (March 10, 1967): 1203–7. See also Harvey Cox, *The Secular City* (New York: Macmillan Co., paperback, 1965), pp. 17–37, who characterizes the Genesis accounts from the standpoint of the surrounding faiths as "atheistic propaganda" (p. 23).

36. See Robert Gordis, *Koheleth* (New York: Schocken Books, paperback, 1968), pp. 116–17, for this interpretation of Job.

37. Bertrand Russell, *Religion and Science* (New York: Oxford University Press, Galaxy Books, 1961), pp. 221–22.

38. Some scholars have suggested that this warning was initially formulated with the technological accomplishments and self-confidence of the Solomonic age in mind.

39. By the Assyrians (repeatedly in the eighth century) and the Babylonians (sixth century), domination by the Persians (sixth through fourth centuries), then invasion by the Greeks (fourth century) and the Romans (first century). Examples of the savagery of the Assyrian assaults upon the cities of Syro-Palestine may be seen in various historical texts (*ANET*, pp. 276–301).

40. Paul Hanson, *The Dawn of Apocalyptic* (Philadelphia: Fortress Press, 1975) for evidence in the postexilic prophets.

41. Graphic details may be found in the writings of the Jewish historian Josephus (first century A.D.).

42. The beginnings of this mentality are already evident in the protoapocalyptic literature of the OT (see chap. 3, sec. G, above).

43. Russell, *Religion and Science*, p. 81.

44. Ernest Becker, *The Denial of Death* (New York: Macmillan Co., Free Press, 1973), pp. 282–83.

45. Martin Heidegger, *Sein und Zeit* (Halle: Max Niemeyer Verlag, 1927). For a relatively clear exposition and trenchant criticism see Walter Kaufmann, "Existentialism and Death," in *The Meaning of Death*, ed. Feifel, pp. 39–63.

46. Jean-Paul Sartre, *Being and Nothingness* (New York: Philosophical Library, 1956), pp. 537, 539.

47. Hans Morgenthau, "Death in the Nuclear Age," in *The Modern Vision of Death*, ed. Nathan Scott, Jr. (Richmond: John Knox Press, 1967), p. 77.

48. See Arthur McGill, "Death as Destruction and Nourishment," (an unpublished paper presented to the American Theological Society, April 4–5, 1975), pp. 27–30.

49. See also chap. 3, sec. F.

50. See Bailey, "Mortality and the Fear of Death," p. 257.

51. The English translations usually read, "We will not die," following the present MT. However, Rabbinic literature contains a list of passages *(tiqqune-sopherim)* where an earlier reading has been remembered, this text among them. Presumably, even to assert that God was not subject to death was considered offensive in that a hypothetical question about it could be raised. Hence the change of reading. In general see C. McCarthy, "Emendations of the Scribes," *IDBS*.

52. For a brief but adequate statement of the two perspectives, favoring the latter, see Paul Hoon, "Theology, Death, and the Funeral Liturgy," *USQR* 31 (1976): 169–81.

53. Ibid., p. 175, for the assertion that these emphases are the proper ones.

54. Ibid., p. 177, for this observation and suggestion.

55. As contained in *Proposed Revisions for the Book of Worship* (Nash-

ville: Methodist Publishing House, 1960), pp. 49-60. I have chosen this church's liturgy for illustration solely because it is my own denomination.

56. The other readings will likely now be interpreted by the congregation in the light of this initial one, which may result in some distortion of the texts. For example, "underneath are the everlasting arms" (Deut. 33:27) belongs initially in the context of protection in battle˙

57 Including such mistranslations as "the shadow of death" (Ps. 23:4) and such surely-to-be-misunderstood passages as "dwell in the house of the Lord forever" (Ps. 23:6), which refers only to lifelong worship in the temple in Jerusalem.

58. Dempsey, *The Way We Die,* chap. 7 ("We Who Now Mourn and Weep"), esp. pp. 158-66.

59. Ibid., p. 164, citing the casework of Kübler-Ross, who has advocated that hospitals need to have "screaming rooms." My own conversations with persons who have utilized such relatively new facilities indicate that it is therapeutic.

60. Schuyler Brown, "Bereavement in New Testament Perspective," *Worship* 48, no. 2, p. 93. For a similar caution see John Meier, "Catholic Funerals in the Light of Scripture," *Worship* 48, no. 4, pp. 206-16.

61. Carl G. Jung, "The Soul and Death," in *The Meaning of Death,* ed. Feifel, p. 6.

62. For death as the moment of decision see Ladislaus Boros, *The Moment of Truth* (London: Burns and Oates, 1965); Karl Rahner, *On the Theology of Death* (New York: Herder & Herder, 1961); and Gisbert Greshake, "Towards a Theology of Dying," in *The Experience of Dying,* ed. Greinacher and Müller, pp. 80-98.

63. See especially Greshake, "Towards a Theology of Dying," and the literature cited there. In general Roman Catholic writers seem to have been more concerned with this theological problem than have Protestants.

# Indexes

## ANCIENT SOURCES

## AUTHORS

Trible, Phyllis, 132
Tromp, Nicolas, 37, 42, 124, 130
Turner, N., 137

Vawter, Bruce, 122, 126
Vermes, Geza, 139
Virgil, 114
Volz, Paul, 124
Vyver, Frank de, 142

Wakeman, Mary, 132

Weiser, Artur, 60, 134
Westermann, Claus, 133, 135
White, Lynn, Jr., 145
Wolff, H. W., 33, 122, 126, 129,
 130, 133, 135
Wolff, Hope, 124
Wrightsman, Lawrence, 102,
 144

Zeitlin, Solomon, 137
Zimmerli, Walther, 132, 135

## SUBJECTS

"Adam" (not a proper name),
 128
Amulets, 11, 14
Anat (goddess), 27
Ancestor cult, 32, 127
Anthropology, Israelite, 41–44,
 77–78, 98
Anunnaki (deities), 19
Apollo (deity), 15
Aqhat Epic, 27, 123
Aralu (underworld), 19
Ars moriendi (literature), 114
Arslan Tash (site), 14
Ashurbanipal (king), 11
Atrahasis Epic, 5, 12, 17, 115,
 130
Autopsies, 101

Baal Epic, 65
Bioethics, 97–101

Childlessness, 49–51
Counseling, 97–101, 143
Cremation, 101

Cryonics, 112

Death angel, 134
Demons, 8–9, 12–15, 28–32, 57,
 75, 116, 117, 118
Devil (*see also* Satan), 15, 82, 129
Dumuzi (Tammuz), 7

Ea (deity), 6, 12
El (deity), 8, 15
Elysian Fields, 136
Enemy, death as, 88–89, 93, 134
Enkidu, 7, 10, 17–18
Enlil (deity), 5
Enuma Elish Epic, 6, 17, 123
Ereshkigal (deity), 19
Eschatology, apocalyptic, 63,
 67–74, 75, 87, 134
Eschatology, prophetic, 63–67,
 134
Eschatology, "realized," 87, 138
Etiology, 36–39, 87, 128, 132
Execution, 49, 100
Existentialism, 112, 113

## WORDS